Precious Bible Promises

PRECIOUS BIBLE PROMISES

From the
New King James Version

THOMAS NELSON PUBLISHERS
Nashville • Camden • New York

Published in Nashville, Tennessee, by Thomas Nelson, Inc., and distributed in Canada by Lawson Falle, Ltd., Cambridge, Ontario.

Printed in the United States of America.

ISBN 0-8407-3153-1 BURGUNDY

17 18 19 20 - 93 92 91 90

Introduction

Centuries before the Bible was completed, the psalmist wrote, "Your word is a lamp to my feet and a light to my path" (Ps. 119:105). That same esteem of the Word of God continues to be shared by millions in the midst of the sin and confusion of today, serving Christians as a light by which to walk through the darkness of this world.

Someone has said that there are more than thirty-seven thousand promises in the Word of God. *Precious Bible Promises* makes the most prominent of those readily available in a systematic form. The themes covered relate to the most vital needs in everyday living.

The book is designed for use in personal devotions and will also be effective when used by pastors and other Christian workers in counseling, hospital and shut-in visitation, and in other situations where one requires Bible passages arranged thematically in a convenient format.

Contents

How precious also are Your thoughts
to me, O God!
How great is the sum of them!

PSALM 139:17

The Bible— Our Source Book

All Scripture is given by inspiration of God, and is profitable for doctrine, for reproof, for correction, for instruction in righteousness,

That the man of God may be complete, thoroughly equipped for every good work.

2 TIMOTHY 3:16–17

"You search the Scriptures, for in them you think you have eternal life; and these are they which testify of Me." JOHN 5:39

Knowing this first, that no prophecy of Scripture is of any private interpretation,

for prophecy never came by the will of man, but holy men of God spoke as they were moved by the Holy Spirit. 2 PETER 1:20–21

"Therefore whoever hears these sayings of Mine, and does them, I will liken him to a wise man who built his house on the rock:

"and the rain descended, the floods came,

and the winds blew and beat on that house; and it did not fall, for it was founded on the rock."

MATTHEW 7:24–25

"He who rejects Me, and does not receive My words, has that which judges him—the word that I have spoken will judge him in the last day.

"For I have not spoken on My own authority; but the Father who sent Me gave Me a command, what I should say and what I should speak.

"And I know that His command is everlasting life. Therefore, whatever I speak, just as the Father has told Me, so I speak."

JOHN 12:48–50

"Most assuredly, I say to you, he who hears My word and believes in Him who sent Me has everlasting life, and shall not come into judgment, but has passed from death into life."

JOHN 5:24

Every word of God is pure; He is a shield to those who put their trust in Him.

Do not add to His words, lest He reprove you, and you be found a liar. PROVERBS 30:5–6

By the word of the Lord the heavens were made, and all the host of them by the breath of His mouth. PSALM 33:6

I will worship toward Your holy temple, and praise Your name for Your lovingkindness and Your truth; for You have magnified Your word above all Your name. PSALM 138:2

For the word of God is living and powerful, and sharper than any two-edged sword, piercing even to the division of soul and spirit, and of joints and marrow, and is a discerner of the thoughts and intents of the heart.

HEBREWS 4:12

Let all the earth fear the Lord; let all the inhabitants of the world stand in awe of Him.
For He spoke, and it was done; He commanded, and it stood fast. PSALM 33:8–9

For I testify to everyone who hears the words of the prophecy of this book: If anyone adds to these things, God will add to him the plagues that are written in this book;
and if anyone takes away from the words of the book of this prophecy, God shall take away his part from the Book of Life, from the

holy city, and from the things which are written in this book." REVELATION 22:18–19

"And now, brethren, I commend you to God and to the word of His grace, which is able to build you up and give you an inheritance among all those who are sanctified." ACTS 20:32

"Heaven and earth will pass away, but My words will by no means pass away." MARK 13:31

"For as the rain comes down, and the snow from heaven, and do not return there, but water the earth, and make it bring forth and bud, that it may give seed to the sower and bread to the eater,

So shall My word be that goes forth from My mouth; it shall not return to Me void, but it shall accomplish what I please, and it shall prosper in the thing for which I sent it."

ISAIAH 55:10–11

"Blessed be the Lord, who has given rest to His people Israel, according to all that He promised. There has not failed one word of all His good promise, which He promised through His servant Moses." 1 KINGS 8:56

My son, give attention to my words; incline your ear to my sayings.

Do not let them depart from your eyes; keep them in the midst of your heart;

For they are life to those who find them, and health to all their flesh. PROVERBS 4:20–22

The Bible—Our Comfort

For whatever things were written before were written for our learning, that we through the patience and comfort of the Scriptures might have hope. ROMANS 15:4

God is our refuge and strength, a very present help in trouble. PSALM 46:1

And these things we write to you that your joy may be full. 1 JOHN 1:4

My son, do not forget my law, but let your heart keep my commands;

For length of days and long life and peace they will add to you. PROVERBS 3:1–2

But as it is written: "Eye has not seen, nor ear heard, nor have entered into the heart of man the things which God has prepared for those who love Him." 1 CORINTHIANS 2:9

My son, give attention to my words; incline your ear to my sayings.

Do not let them depart from your eyes; keep them in the midst of your heart;

For they are life to those who find them, and health to all their flesh. PROVERBS 4:20–22

This is my comfort in my affliction, for Your word has given me life. PSALM 119:50

Unless Your law had been my delight, I would then have perished in my affliction.
PSALM 119:92

So then faith comes by hearing, and hearing by the word of God. ROMANS 10:17

The law of the Lord is perfect, converting the soul; the testimony of the Lord is sure, making wise the simple;

The statutes of the Lord are right, rejoicing the heart; the commandment of the Lord is pure, enlightening the eyes. PSALM 19:7–8

I will never forget Your precepts, for by them You have given me life. PSALM 119:93

Therefore lay aside all filthiness and overflow of wickedness, and receive with meekness the implanted word, which is able to save your souls.

He who looks into the perfect law of liberty and continues in it, and is not a forgetful hearer but a doer of the work, this one will be blessed in what he does. JAMES 1:21,25

Great peace have those who love Your law, and nothing causes them to stumble.

PSALM 119:165

"For as the rain comes down, and the snow from heaven, and do not return there, but water the earth, and make it bring forth and bud, that it may give seed to the sower and bread to the eater,

So shall My word be that goes forth from My mouth; it shall not return to Me void, but it shall accomplish what I please, and it shall prosper in the thing for which I sent it."

ISAIAH 55:10–11

"If you keep My commandments, you will

abide in My love, just as I have kept My Father's commandments and abide in His love.

"These things I have spoken to you, that My joy may remain in you, and that your joy may be full." JOHN 15:10–11

And if you are Christ's, then you are Abraham's seed, and heirs according to the promise. GALATIANS 3:29

"In My Father's house are many mansions; if it were not so, I would have told you. I go to prepare a place for you.

"And if I go and prepare a place for you, I will come again and receive you to Myself; that where I am, there you may be also." JOHN 14:2–3

Then the King will say to those on His right hand, "Come, you blessed of My Father, inherit the kingdom prepared for you from the foundation of the world." MATTHEW 25:34

Now to Him who is able to keep you from stumbling, and to present you faultless before the presence of His glory with exceeding joy,

To God our Savior, who alone is wise, be glory and majesty, dominion and power, both now and forever. Amen. JUDE 24–25

Every word of God is pure; He is a shield to those who put their trust in Him.

PROVERBS 30:5

The Bible—Our Guide

"This Book of the Law shall not depart from your mouth, but you shall meditate in it day and night, that you may observe to do according to all that is written in it. For then you will make your way prosperous, and then you will have good success." JOSHUA 1:8

Then Jesus said to those Jews who believed Him, "If you abide in My word, you are My disciples indeed.

"And you shall know the truth, and the truth shall make you free." JOHN 8:31–32

All Scripture is given by inspiration of God, and is profitable for doctrine, for reproof, for correction, for instruction in righteousness,

that the man of God may be complete, thoroughly equipped for every good work.

2 TIMOTHY 3:16–17

When you roam, they will lead you; when you sleep, they will keep you; and when you awake, they will speak with you.

For the commandment is a lamp, and the law is light; reproofs of instruction are the way of life. PROVERBS 6:22–23

Your word is a lamp to my feet and a light to my path. PSALM 119:105

Trust in the Lord with all your heart, and lean not on your own understanding;

In all your ways acknowledge Him, and He shall direct your paths. PROVERBS 3:5–6

The law of the Lord is perfect, converting the soul; the testimony of the Lord is sure, making wise the simple.

More to be desired are they than gold, yea, than much fine gold; sweeter also than honey and the honeycomb.

Moreover by them Your servant is warned, and in keeping them there is great reward.

PSALM 19:7,10–11

Your ears shall hear a word behind you, saying, "This is the way, walk in it," whenever you turn to the right hand or whenever you turn to the left. ISAIAH 30:21

How can a young man cleanse his way? By taking heed according to Your word.

Your word I have hidden in my heart, that I might not sin against You. PSALM 119:9,11

He spoke by the mouth of His holy prophets, who have been since the world began.

To give light to those who sit in darkness and the shadow of death, to guide our feet into the way of peace. LUKE 1:70,79

Your testimonies also are my delight and my counselors. PSALM 119:24

Nevertheless I am continually with You; You hold me by my right hand.

You will guide me with Your counsel, and afterward receive me to glory. PSALM 73:23–24

If any of you lacks wisdom, let him ask of God, who gives to all liberally and without reproach, and it will be given to him. JAMES 1:5

Wait on the Lord, and keep His way, and

He shall exalt you to inherit the land; when the wicked are cut off, you shall see it. PSALM 37:34

The steps of a good man are ordered by the Lord, and He delights in his way.
Though he fall, he shall not be utterly cast down; for the Lord upholds him with His hand.
PSALM 37:23–24

I will instruct you and teach you in the way you should go; I will guide you with My eye.
PSALM 32:8

"For You are my lamp, O Lord; the Lord shall enlighten my darkness." 2 SAMUEL 22:29

For You are my rock and my fortress; therefore, for Your name's sake, lead me and guide me. PSALM 31:3

The Bible—Our Strength

Having been born again, not of corruptible seed but incorruptible, through the word of God which lives and abides forever. 1 PETER 1:23

"And now, brethren, I commend you to God and to the word of His grace, which is able to build you up and give you an inheritance among all those who are sanctified." ACTS 20:32

Now He who establishes us with you in Christ and has anointed us is God,
who also has sealed us and given us the Spirit in our hearts as a deposit.

2 CORINTHIANS 1:21–22

Because "All flesh is as grass, and all the glory of man as the flower of the grass. The grass withers, and its flower falls away,
But the word of the Lord endures forever."
Now this is the word which by the gospel was preached to you. 1 PETER 1:24–25

"Blessed be the Lord, who has given rest to His people Israel, according to all that He promised. There has not failed one word of all His good promise, which He promised through His servant Moses." 1 KINGS 8:56

"And it is easier for heaven and earth to pass away than for one tittle of the law to fail."

LUKE 16:17

The counsel of the Lord stands forever, the plans of His heart to all generations. PSALM 33:11

The works of His hands are verity and justice; all His precepts are sure.

They stand fast forever and ever, and are done in truth and uprightness. PSALM 111:7–8

"Heaven and earth will pass away, but My words will by no means pass away." MARK 13:31

Forever, O Lord, Your word is settled in heaven. PSALM 119:89

In Him you also trusted, after you heard the word of truth, the gospel of your salvation; in whom also, having believed, you were sealed with the Holy Spirit of promise,

who is the guarantee of our inheritance until the redemption of the purchased possession, to the praise of His glory.

EPHESIANS 1:13–14

As for God, His way is perfect; the word of the Lord is proven; He is a shield to all who trust in Him. PSALM 18:30

The eternal God is your refuge, and underneath are the everlasting arms; He will thrust out the enemy from before you, and will say, "Destroy!" DEUTERONOMY 33:27

"For assuredly, I say to you, till heaven and earth pass away, one jot or one tittle will by no means pass from the law till all is fulfilled."

MATTHEW 5:18

For thus says the Lord God, the Holy One of Israel: "In returning and rest you shall be saved; in quietness and confidence shall be your strength." ISAIAH 30:15

My soul melts from heaviness; strengthen me according to Your word. PSALM 119:28

But those who wait on the Lord shall renew their strength; they shall mount up with wings like eagles, they shall run and not be weary, they shall walk and not faint. ISAIAH 40:31

PROMISES OF SALVATION

The Need for Salvation

For the wrath of God is revealed from heaven against all ungodliness and unrighteousness of men, who suppress the truth in unrighteousness.

Because, although they knew God, they did not glorify Him as God, nor were thankful, but became futile in their thoughts, and their foolish hearts were darkened. ROMANS 1:18,21

The Lord is not slack concerning His promise, as some count slackness, but is longsuffering toward us, not willing that any should perish but that all should come to repentance. 2 PETER 3:9

What then? Are we better than they? Not at all. For we have previously charged both Jews and Greeks that they are all under sin.

As it is written: "There is none righteous, no, not one;

"There is none who understands; there is none who seeks after God.

"They have all gone out of the way; they have together become unprofitable; there is none who does good, no, not one." ROMANS 3:9–12

Jesus answered and said to him, "Most assuredly, I say to you, unless one is born again, he cannot see the kingdom of God."

JOHN 3:3

"Truly, these times of ignorance God overlooked, but now commands all men everywhere to repent,

"because He has appointed a day on which He will judge the world in righteousness by the Man whom He has ordained. He has given assurance of this to all by raising Him from the dead." ACTS 17:30–31

For all have sinned and fall short of the glory of God. ROMANS 3:23

And in them the prophecy of Isaiah is fulfilled, which says: "Hearing you will hear and shall not understand, and seeing you will see and not perceive;

"For the heart of this people has grown dull. Their ears are hard of hearing, and their eyes they have closed, lest they should see with their eyes and hear with their ears, lest they should understand with their heart and turn, so that I should heal them." MATTHEW 13:14–15

For the wages of sin is death, but the gift of God is eternal life in Christ Jesus our Lord.

ROMANS 6:23

But in accordance with your hardness and your impenitent heart you are treasuring up for yourself wrath in the day of wrath and revelation of the righteous judgment of God.

ROMANS 2:5

For to be carnally minded is death, but to be spiritually minded is life and peace.

Because the carnal mind is enmity against God; for it is not subject to the law of God, nor indeed can be.

So then, those who are in the flesh cannot please God. ROMANS 8:6–8

There is a way which seems right to a man, but its end is the way of death. PROVERBS 14:12

For many walk, of whom I have told you

often, and now tell you even weeping, that they are the enemies of the cross of Christ:

whose end is destruction, whose god is their belly, and whose glory is in their shame—who set their mind on earthly things.

PHILIPPIANS 3:18–19

O wretched man that I am! Who will deliver me from this body of death?

I thank God—through Jesus Christ our Lord! So then, with the mind I myself serve the law of God, but with the flesh the law of sin.

ROMANS 7:24–25

Let no one deceive you with empty words, for because of these things the wrath of God comes upon the sons of disobedience.

EPHESIANS 5:6

Therefore put to death your members which are on the earth: fornication, uncleanness, passion, evil desire, and covetousness, which is idolatry.

Because of these things the wrath of God is coming upon the sons of disobedience.

COLOSSIANS 3:5–6

The Provision of Salvation

"For God so loved the world that He gave His only begotten Son, that whoever believes in Him should not perish but have everlasting life."

JOHN 3:16

"God has fulfilled this for us their children, in that He has raised up Jesus. As it is also written in the second Psalm: 'You are My Son, today I have begotten You.'

"Therefore let it be known to you, brethren, that through this Man is preached to you the forgiveness of sins." ACTS 13:33,38

In Him we have redemption through His blood, the forgiveness of sins, according to the riches of His grace. EPHESIANS 1:7

"For God did not send His Son into the world to condemn the world, but that the world through Him might be saved." JOHN 3:17

But now the righteousness of God apart from the law is revealed, being witnessed by the Law and the Prophets,

even the righteousness of God which is

through faith in Jesus Christ to all and on all who believe. For there is no difference.
ROMANS 3:21–22

"For the Son of Man has come to seek and to save that which was lost." LUKE 19:10

Being justified freely by His grace through the redemption that is in Christ Jesus,
whom God set forth to be a propitiation by His blood, through faith, to demonstrate His righteousness, because in His forbearance God had passed over the sins that were previously committed. ROMANS 3:24–25

"Him God has exalted to His right hand to be Prince and Savior, to give repentance to Israel and forgiveness of sins." ACTS 5:31

For I delivered to you first of all that which I also received: that Christ died for our sins according to the Scriptures. 1 CORINTHIANS 15:3

For when we were still without strength, in due time Christ died for the ungodly.
For scarcely for a righteous man will one

die; yet perhaps for a good man someone would even dare to die.'

But God demonstrates His own love toward us, in that while we were still sinners, Christ died for us. ROMANS 5:6–8

And we know that the Son of God has come and has given us an understanding, that we may know Him who is true; and we are in Him who is true, in His Son Jesus Christ. This is the true God and eternal life. 1 JOHN 5:20

For it is the God who commanded light to shine out of darkness who has shone in our hearts to give the light of the knowledge of the glory of God in the face of Jesus Christ.

2 CORINTHIANS 4:6

For if when we were enemies we were reconciled to God through the death of His Son, much more, having been reconciled, we shall be saved by His life. ROMANS 5:10

And Jesus answered and said to him, "Get behind Me, Satan! For it is written, 'You shall worship the Lord your God, and Him only you shall serve.'" LUKE 4:8

"And she will bring forth a Son, and you shall call His name Jesus, for He will save His people from their sins." MATTHEW 1:21

The Grace of God

Not by works of righteousness which we have done, but according to His mercy He saved us, through the washing of regeneration and renewing of the Holy Spirit. TITUS 3:5

For by grace you have been saved through faith, and that not of yourselves; it is the gift of God. EPHESIANS 2:8

Who has saved us and called us with a holy calling, not according to our works, but according to His own purpose and grace which was given to us in Christ Jesus before time began. 2 TIMOTHY 1:9

For the Lord God is a sun and shield; the Lord will give grace and glory; no good thing will He withhold from those who walk uprightly.

PSALM 84:11

To the praise of the glory of His grace, by which He has made us accepted in the Beloved.

EPHESIANS 1:6

Let us therefore come boldly to the throne of grace, that we may obtain mercy and find grace to help in time of need. HEBREWS 4:16

"The sons of foreigners shall build up your walls, and their kings shall minister to you; for in My wrath I struck you, but in My favor I have had mercy on you." ISAIAH 60:10

"Then I will give them a heart to know Me, that I am the Lord; and they shall be My people, and I will be their God, for they shall return to Me with their whole heart." JEREMIAH 24:7

"Then I will give them one heart, and I will put a new spirit within them, and take the stony heart out of their flesh, and give them a heart of flesh,

"that they may walk in My statutes and keep My judgments and do them; and they shall be My people, and I will be their God."

EZEKIEL 11:19–20

For sin shall not have dominion over you, for you are not under law but under grace.
ROMANS 6:14

"But we believe that through the grace of the Lord Jesus Christ we shall be saved in the same manner as they." ACTS 15:11

Being justified freely by His grace through the redemption that is in Christ Jesus,
whom God set forth to be a propitiation by His blood, through faith, to demonstrate His righteousness, because in His forbearance God had passed over the sins that were previously committed. ROMANS 3:24–25

But the free gift is not like the offense. For if by the one man's offense many died, much more the grace of God and the gift by the grace of the one Man, Jesus Christ, abounded to many. ROMANS 5:15

Conviction

The sacrifices of God are a broken spirit, a broken and a contrite heart—these, O God, You will not despise. PSALM 51:17

And the tax collector, standing afar off, would not so much as raise his eyes to heaven, but beat his breast, saying, "God be merciful to me a sinner!" LUKE 18:13

"Nevertheless I tell you the truth. It is to your advantage that I go away; for if I do not go away, the Helper will not come to you; but if I depart, I will send Him to you.

"And when He has come, He will convict the world of sin, and of righteousness, and of judgment:

"of sin, because they do not believe in Me;

"of righteousness, because I go to My Father and you see Me no more;

"of judgment, because the ruler of this world is judged." JOHN 16:7–11

Then I said: "Woe is me, for I am undone! Because I am a man of unclean lips, and I dwell in the midst of a people of unclean lips; for my eyes have seen the King, the Lord of hosts."

ISAIAH 6:5

Who show the work of the law written in their hearts, their conscience also bearing witness, and between themselves their thoughts accusing or else excusing them. ROMANS 2:15

Now when they heard this, they were cut to the heart, and said to Peter and the rest of the apostles, "Men and brethren, what shall we do?"

ACTS 2:37

Then the eyes of both of them were opened, and they knew that they were naked; and they sewed fig leaves together and made themselves coverings.

And they heard the sound of the Lord God walking in the garden in the cool of the day, and Adam and his wife hid themselves from the presence of the Lord God among the trees of the garden. GENESIS 3:7–8

For I acknowledge my transgressions, and my sin is ever before me.

Against You, You only, have I sinned, and done this evil in Your sight—that You may be found just when You speak, and blameless when You judge. PSALM 51:3–4

"See, O Lord, that I am in distress; my soul is troubled; my heart is overturned within me, for I have been very rebellious. Outside the sword bereaves, at home it is like death."

LAMENTATIONS 1:20

When Simon Peter saw it, he fell down at Jesus' knees, saying, "Depart from me, for I am a sinful man, O Lord!" LUKE 5:8

"Behold, I am vile; what shall I answer You? I lay my hand over my mouth.

"Once I have spoken, but I will not answer; yes, twice, but I will proceed no further."

JOB 40:4–5

But if all prophesy, and an unbeliever or an uninformed person comes in, he is convinced by all, he is judged by all.

And thus the secrets of his heart are revealed; and so, falling down on his face, he will worship God and report that God is truly among you. 1 CORINTHIANS 14:24–25

Then he called for a light, ran in, and fell down trembling before Paul and Silas.

And he brought them out and said, "Sirs, what must I do to be saved?" ACTS 16:29–30

For my life is spent with grief, and my years with sighing; my strength fails because of my iniquity, and my bones waste away. PSALM 31:10

Then call, and I will answer; or let me speak, then You respond to me.

How many are my iniquities and sins? Make me know my transgression and my sin.

JOB 13:22–23

Then they said to one another, "We are truly guilty concerning our brother, for we saw the anguish of his soul when he pleaded with us, and we would not hear; therefore this distress has come upon us."

And Reuben answered them, saying, "Did I not speak to you, saying, 'Do not sin against the boy'; and you would not listen? Therefore behold, his blood is now required of us."

GENESIS 42:21–22

Faith

For by grace you have been saved through faith, and that not of yourselves; it is the gift of God. EPHESIANS 2:8

So they said, "Believe on the Lord Jesus Christ, and you will be saved, you and your household." ACTS 16:31

"He who believes and is baptized will be saved; but he who does not believe will be condemned." MARK 16:16

That if you confess with your mouth the Lord Jesus and believe in your heart that God has raised Him from the dead, you will be saved.

For with the heart one believes to righteousness, and with the mouth confession is made to salvation. ROMANS 10:9–10

"To Him all the prophets witness that, through His name, whoever believes in Him will receive remission of sins." ACTS 10:43

But without faith it is impossible to please Him, for he who comes to God must believe that He is, and that He is a rewarder of those who diligently seek Him. HEBREWS 11:6

So then faith comes by hearing, and hearing by the word of God. ROMANS 10:17

For whatever is born of God overcomes the world. And this is the victory that has overcome the world—our faith.

Who is he who overcomes the world, but he who believes that Jesus is the Son of God?

1 JOHN 5:4–5

Now when the Gentiles heard this, they were glad and glorified the word of the Lord. And as many as had been appointed to eternal life believed. ACTS 13:48

Then Philip said, "If you believe with all your heart, you may." And he answered and said, "I believe that Jesus Christ is the Son of God." ACTS 8:37

Then many came to Him and said, "John performed no sign, but all the things that John spoke about this Man were true."

And many believed in Him there.

JOHN 10:41–42

Jesus said to her, "I am the resurrection and the life. He who believes in Me, though he may die, he shall live." JOHN 11:25

Then He said to the woman, "Your faith has saved you. Go in peace." LUKE 7:50

But when they believed Philip as he preached the things concerning the kingdom of God and the name of Jesus Christ, both men and women were baptized. ACTS 8:12

"Believe Me that I am in the Father and the Father in Me, or else believe Me for the sake of the works themselves.

"Most assuredly, I say to you, he who believes in Me, the works that I do he will do also; and greater works than these he will do, because I go to My Father." JOHN 14:11–12

The centurion answered and said, "Lord, I am not worthy that You should come under my roof. But only speak a word, and my servant will be healed.

"For I also am a man under authority, having soldiers under me. And I say to this one, 'Go,' and he goes; and to another, 'Come,' and he comes; and to my servant, 'Do this,' and he does it."

When Jesus heard it, He marveled, and said to those who followed, "Assuredly, I say to you, I have not found such great faith, not even in Israel!" MATTHEW 8:8–10

Then he said to Jesus, "Lord, remember me when You come into Your kingdom."

And Jesus said to him, "Assuredly, I say to you, today you will be with Me in Paradise."

LUKE 23:42–43

For to you it has been granted on behalf of Christ, not only to believe in Him, but also to suffer for His sake. PHILIPPIANS 1:29

And suddenly, a woman who had a flow of blood for twelve years came from behind and touched the hem of His garment;

for she said to herself, "If only I may touch His garment, I shall be made well."

But Jesus turned around, and when He saw her He said, "Be of good cheer, daughter; your faith has made you well." And the woman was made well from that hour. MATTHEW 9:20–22

Repentance

Then Peter said to them, "Repent, and let every one of you be baptized in the name of Jesus Christ for the remission of sins; and you shall receive the gift of the Holy Spirit.

"For the promise is to you and to your children, and to all who are afar off, as many as the Lord our God will call." ACTS 2:38–39

"I have not come to call the righteous, but sinners, to repentance." LUKE 5:32

Or do you despise the riches of His goodness, forbearance, and longsuffering, not knowing that the goodness of God leads you to repentance? ROMANS 2:4

The Lord is not slack concerning His promise, as some count slackness, but is longsuffering toward us, not willing that any should perish but that all should come to repentance. 2 PETER 3:9

If we say that we have no sin, we deceive ourselves, and the truth is not in us.
If we confess our sins, He is faithful and just to forgive us our sins and to cleanse us from all unrighteousness. 1 JOHN 1:8–9

"Repent therefore and be converted, that your sins may be blotted out, so that times of refreshing may come from the presence of the Lord." ACTS 3:19

Draw near to God and He will draw near to you. Cleanse your hands, you sinners; and purify your hearts, you double-minded.

Lament and mourn and weep! Let your laughter be turned to mourning and your joy to gloom.

Humble yourselves in the sight of the Lord, and He will lift you up. JAMES 4:8–10

"The men of Nineveh will rise in the judgment with this generation and condemn it, because they repented at the preaching of Jonah; and indeed a greater than Jonah is here." MATTHEW 12:41

"And it shall come to pass that whoever calls on the name of the Lord shall be saved."
ACTS 2:21

"Repent, for the kingdom of heaven is at hand!" MATTHEW 3:2

For you were like sheep going astray, but have now returned to the Shepherd and Overseer of your souls. 1 PETER 2:25

Now I rejoice, not that you were made sorry, but that your sorrow led to repentance. For you were made sorry in a godly manner, that you might suffer loss from us in nothing.

2 CORINTHIANS 7:9

For you know that afterward, when he wanted to inherit the blessing, he was rejected, for he found no place for repentance, though he sought it diligently with tears. HEBREWS 12:17

Seek good and not evil, that you may live; so the Lord God of hosts will be with you, as you have spoken. AMOS 5:14

"Woe to you, Chorazin! Woe to you, Bethsaida! For if the mighty works which were done in you had been done in Tyre and Sidon, they would have repented a great while ago, sitting in sackcloth and ashes." LUKE 10:13

Thus says the Lord of hosts, the God of Israel: "Amend your ways and your doings, and I will cause you to dwell in this place.

"Do not trust in these lying words, saying, 'The temple of the Lord, the temple of the Lord, the temple of the Lord are these.'

"For if you thoroughly amend your ways and your doings, if you thoroughly execute judgment between a man and his neighbor,

"if you do not oppress the stranger, the fatherless, and the widow, and do not shed innocent blood in this place, or walk after other gods to your hurt,

"then I will cause you to dwell in this place, in the land that I gave to your fathers forever and ever." JEREMIAH 7:3–7

Confession

❧ If you confess with your mouth the Lord Jesus and believe in your heart that God has raised Him from the dead, you will be saved.

For with the heart one believes to righteousness, and with the mouth confession is made to salvation. ROMANS 10:9–10

"Therefore whoever confesses Me before men, him I will also confess before My Father who is in heaven." MATTHEW 10:32

Confess your trespasses to one another, and pray for one another, that you may be healed. The effective, fervent prayer of a righteous man avails much. JAMES 5:16

If we confess our sins, He is faithful and just to forgive us our sins and to cleanse us from all unrighteousness. 1 JOHN 1:9

I acknowledged my sin to You, and my iniquity I have not hidden. I said, "I will confess my transgressions to the Lord," and You forgave the iniquity of my sin. PSALM 32:5

Then I heard a loud voice saying in heaven, "Now salvation, and strength, and the kingdom of our God, and the power of His Christ have come, for the accuser of our brethren, who accused them before our God day and night, has been cast down.

"And they overcame him by the blood of the Lamb and by the word of their testimony, and they did not love their lives to the death."

REVELATION 12:10–11

Let us hold fast the confession of our hope without wavering, for He who promised is faithful. HEBREWS 10:23

Deliver me from bloodguiltiness, O God, the God of my salvation, and my tongue shall sing aloud of Your righteousness.

O Lord, open my lips, and my mouth shall show forth Your praise. PSALM 51:14–15

Through the proof of this ministry, they glorify God for the obedience of your confession to the gospel of Christ, and for your liberal sharing with them and all men.

2 CORINTHIANS 9:13

"Also I say to you, whoever confesses Me before men, him the Son of Man also will confess before the angels of God." LUKE 12:8

And all the land of Judea, and those from Jerusalem, went out to him and were all baptized by him in the Jordan River, confessing their sins. MARK 1:5

Therefore I make known to you that no one speaking by the Spirit of God calls Jesus accursed, and no one can say that Jesus is Lord except by the Holy Spirit.

1 CORINTHIANS 12:3

And that every tongue should confess that Jesus Christ is Lord, to the glory of God the Father. PHILIPPIANS 2:11

You have put gladness in my heart, more than in the season that their grain and wine increased. PSALM 4:7

I will greatly rejoice in the Lord, my soul shall be joyful in God; for He has clothed me with the garments of salvation, He has covered me with the robe of righteousness, as a bridegroom decks himself with ornaments, and as a bride adorns herself with her jewels.

ISAIAH 61:10

The voice of rejoicing and salvation is in the tents of the righteous; the right hand of the Lord does valiantly. PSALM 118:15

So the ransomed of the Lord shall return, and come to Zion with singing, with everlasting joy on their heads; they shall obtain joy and gladness, and sorrow and sighing shall flee away. ISAIAH 51:11

Yet I will rejoice in the Lord, I will joy in the God of my salvation. HABAKKUK 3:18

Acceptance

"All that the Father gives Me will come to Me, and the one who comes to Me I will by no means cast out." JOHN 6:37

"Come now, and let us reason together," says the Lord, "Though your sins are like scarlet, they shall be as white as snow; though they are red like crimson, they shall be as wool." ISAIAH 1:18

"I will cleanse them from all their iniquity by which they have sinned against Me, and I will pardon all their iniquities by which they have sinned and by which they have transgressed against Me." JEREMIAH 33:8

For the Scripture says, "Whoever believes on Him will not be put to shame." ROMANS 10:11

But now in Christ Jesus you who once were far off have been made near by the blood of Christ.

For He Himself is our peace, who has

made both one, and has broken down the middle wall of division between us,

having abolished in His flesh the enmity, that is, the law of commandments contained in ordinances, so as to create in Himself one new man from the two, thus making peace,

and that He might reconcile them both to God in one body through the cross, thereby putting to death the enmity. EPHESIANS 2:13–16

Much more then, having now been justified by His blood, we shall be saved from wrath through Him.

For if when we were enemies we were reconciled to God through the death of His Son, much more, having been reconciled, we shall be saved by His life. ROMANS 5:9–10

Now all things are of God, who has reconciled us to Himself through Jesus Christ, and has given us the ministry of reconciliation,

that is, that God was in Christ reconciling the world to Himself, not imputing their trespasses to them, and has committed to us the word of reconciliation. 2 CORINTHIANS 5:18–19

"But when the wicked turns from his wickedness and does what is lawful and right, he shall live because of it." EZEKIEL 33:19

Coming to Him as to a living stone, rejected indeed by men, but chosen by God and precious,

you also, as living stones, are being built up a spiritual house, a holy priesthood, to offer up spiritual sacrifices acceptable to God through Jesus Christ. 1 PETER 2:4–5

"I, even I, am He who blots out your transgressions for My own sake; and I will not remember your sins." ISAIAH 43:25

"Therefore I say to you, her sins, which are many, are forgiven, for she loved much. But to whom little is forgiven, the same loves little."

And He said to her, "Your sins are forgiven." LUKE 7:47–48

Who is a God like You, pardoning iniquity and passing over the transgression of the remnant of His heritage? He does not retain His anger forever, because He delights in mercy.

He will again have compassion on us, and will subdue our iniquities. You will cast all our sins into the depths of the sea. MICAH 7:18–19

And you, who once were alienated and enemies in your mind by wicked works, yet now He has reconciled

in the body of His flesh through death, to present you holy, and blameless, and irreproachable in His sight—

if indeed you continue in the faith, grounded and steadfast, and are not moved away from the hope of the gospel which you heard, which was preached to every creature under heaven, of which I, Paul, became a minister.

COLOSSIANS 1:21–23

Bless the Lord, O my soul; and all that is within me, bless His holy name!

Bless the Lord, O my soul, and forget not all His benefits:

Who forgives all your iniquities, who heals all your diseases,

Who redeems your life from destruction, who crowns you with lovingkindness and tender mercies,

Who satisfies your mouth with good things, so that your youth is renewed like the eagle's.

PSALM 103:1–5

As far as the east is from the west, so far has He removed our transgressions from us.

As a father pities his children, so the Lord pities those who fear Him. PSALM 103:12–13

For God did not appoint us to wrath, but to obtain salvation through our Lord Jesus Christ,

who died for us, that whether we wake or sleep, we should live together with Him.

1 THESSALONIANS 5:9–10

For "whoever calls upon the name of the Lord shall be saved." ROMANS 10:13

Justification

Blessed is he whose transgression is forgiven, whose sin is covered.

Blessed is the man to whom the Lord does not impute iniquity, and in whose spirit there is no guile. PSALM 32:1–2

That having been justified by His grace we should become heirs according to the hope of eternal life. TITUS 3:7

Therefore, having been justified by faith, we have peace with God through our Lord Jesus Christ. ROMANS 5:1

"By Him everyone who believes is justified from all things from which you could not be justified by the law of Moses." ACTS 13:39

Therefore, as through one man's offense judgment came to all men, resulting in condemnation, even so through one Man's righteous act the free gift came to all men, resulting in justification of life.

For as by one man's disobedience many were made sinners, so also by one Man's obedience many will be made righteous.

ROMANS 5:18–19

"For I will be merciful to their unrighteousness, and their sins and their lawless deeds I will remember no more."

HEBREWS 8:12

And the inhabitant will not say, "I am sick"; the people who dwell in it will be forgiven their iniquity. ISAIAH 33:24

You see then that a man is justified by works, and not by faith only.
Likewise, was not Rahab the harlot also justified by works when she received the messengers and sent them out another way?
For as the body without the spirit is dead, so faith without works is dead also. JAMES 2:24–26

By faith Abel offered to God a more excellent sacrifice than Cain, through which he obtained witness that he was righteous, God testifying of his gifts; and through it he being dead still speaks. HEBREWS 11:4

There is therefore now no condemnation to those who are in Christ Jesus, who do not walk according to the flesh, but according to the Spirit.
Who shall bring a charge against God's elect? It is God who justifies.
Who is he who condemns? It is Christ who died, and furthermore is also risen, who is even

at the right hand of God, who also makes intercession for us. ROMANS 8:1,33–34

"Knowing that a man is not justified by the works of the law but by faith in Jesus Christ, even we have believed in Christ Jesus, that we might be justified by faith in Christ and not by the works of the law; for by the works of the law no flesh shall be justified." GALATIANS 2:16

And you, being dead in your trespasses and the uncircumcision of your flesh, He has made alive together with Him, having forgiven you all trespasses,

having wiped out the handwriting of requirements that was against us, which was contrary to us. And He has taken it out of the way, having nailed it to the cross.

COLOSSIANS 2:13–14

Then He adds, "Their sins and their lawless deeds I will remember no more."

Now where there is remission of these, there is no longer an offering for sin.

HEBREWS 10:17–18

"In the Lord all the descendants of Israel shall be justified, and shall glory." ISAIAH 45:25

Moreover whom He predestined, these He also called; whom He called, these He also justified; and whom He justified, these He also glorified. ROMANS 8:30

Therefore the law was our tutor to bring us to Christ, that we might be justified by faith.
GALATIANS 3:24

Righteousness

For He made Him who knew no sin to be sin for us, that we might become the righteousness of God in Him. 2 CORINTHIANS 5:21

That if you confess with your mouth the Lord Jesus and believe in your heart that God has raised Him from the dead, you will be saved.

For with the heart one believes to righteousness, and with the mouth confession is made to salvation. ROMANS 10:9–10

But indeed I also count all things loss for the excellence of the knowledge of Christ Jesus my Lord, for whom I have suffered the loss of all things, and count them as rubbish, that I may gain Christ

and be found in Him, not having my own righteousness, which is from the law, but that which is through faith in Christ. PHILIPPIANS 3:8–9

For I am not ashamed of the gospel of Christ, for it is the power of God to salvation for everyone who believes, for the Jew first and also for the Greek.

For in it the righteousness of God is revealed from faith to faith; as it is written, "The just shall live by faith." ROMANS 1:16–17

And he believed in the Lord, and He accounted it to him for righteousness.

GENESIS 15:6

"But seek first the kingdom of God and His righteousness, and all these things shall be added to you." MATTHEW 6:33

"Listen to Me, you stubborn-hearted, who are far from righteousness:

"I bring My righteousness near, it shall not be far off; My salvation shall not linger. And I will place salvation in Zion, for Israel My glory."

ISAIAH 46:12–13

By faith Noah, being divinely warned of things not yet seen, moved with godly fear, prepared an ark for the saving of his household, by which he condemned the world and became heir of the righteousness which is according to faith. HEBREWS 11:7

Stand therefore, having girded your waist with truth, having put on the breastplate of righteousness. EPHESIANS 6:14

In Your name they rejoice all day long, and in Your righteousness they are exalted.
PSALM 89:16

He shall say, "Surely in the Lord I have righteousness and strength. To Him men shall come, and all shall be ashamed who are incensed against Him." ISAIAH 45:24

What shall we say then? That Gentiles, who did not pursue righteousness, have attained to righteousness, even the righteousness of faith;

but Israel, pursuing the law of the righteousness, has not attained to the law of righteousness. ROMANS 9:30–31

"Come now, and let us reason together," says the Lord, "Though your sins are like scarlet, they shall be as white as snow; though they are red like crimson, they shall be as wool." ISAIAH 1:18

When Christ who is our life appears, then you also will appear with Him in glory.

Therefore put to death your members which are on the earth: fornication, uncleanness, passion, evil desire, and covetousness, which is idolatry. COLOSSIANS 3:4–5

Therefore if anyone cleanses himself from the latter, he will be a vessel for honor, sanctified and useful for the Master, prepared for every good work.

Flee also youthful lusts; but pursue righteousness, faith, love, peace with those who call on the Lord out of a pure heart.

2 TIMOTHY 2:21–22

For the grace of God that brings salvation has appeared to all men,

teaching us that, denying ungodliness and worldly lusts, we should live soberly, righteously, and godly in the present age, looking for the blessed hope and glorious appearing of our great God and Savior Jesus Christ. TITUS 2:11–13

Was not Abraham our father justified by works when he offered Isaac his son on the altar?

Do you see that faith was working together with his works, and by works faith was made perfect?

And the Scripture was fulfilled which says, "Abraham believed God, and it was accounted to him for righteousness." And he was called the friend of God. JAMES 2:21–23

As obedient children, not conforming yourselves to the former lusts, as in your ignorance;

but as He who called you is holy, you also be holy in all your conduct,

because it is written, "Be holy, for I am holy." 1 PETER 1:14–16

Deliverance

O wretched man that I am! Who will deliver me from this body of death?

I thank God—through Jesus Christ our Lord! ROMANS 7:24–25

There is therefore now no condemnation to those who are in Christ Jesus, who do not walk according to the flesh, but according to the Spirit.

For the law of the Spirit of life in Christ Jesus has made me free from the law of sin and death. ROMANS 8:1–2

Grace to you and peace from God the Father and our Lord Jesus Christ,

who gave Himself for our sins, that He might deliver us from this present evil age, according to the will of our God and Father.

GALATIANS 1:3–4

The angel of the Lord encamps all around those who fear Him, and delivers them.

PSALM 34:7

Knowing this, that our old man was crucified with Him, that the body of sin might be done away with, that we should no longer be slaves of sin.

For sin shall not have dominion over you, for you are not under law but under grace.

ROMANS 6:6,14

"And you shall know the truth, and the truth shall make you free." JOHN 8:32

"For the eyes of the Lord are on the righteous, and his ears are open to their prayers; but the face of the Lord is against those who do evil."

And who is he who will harm you if you become followers of what is good?

1 PETER 3:12–13

But the Lord is faithful, who will establish you and guard you from the evil one.

2 THESSALONIANS 3:3

But know that the Lord has set apart for Himself him who is godly; the Lord will hear when I call to Him. PSALM 4:3

He shall deliver you in six troubles, yes, in seven no evil shall touch you. JOB 5:19

Then the Lord knows how to deliver the godly out of temptations and to reserve the unjust under punishment for the day of judgment. 2 PETER 2:9

"He who believes in Him is not condemned; but he who does not believe is condemned already, because he has not believed in the name of the only begotten Son of God."

JOHN 3:18

For what the law could not do in that it was weak through the flesh, God did by sending His own Son in the likeness of sinful flesh, on account of sin: He condemned sin in the flesh,

that the righteous requirement of the law might be fulfilled in us who do not walk according to the flesh but according to the Spirit. ROMANS 8:3–4

No temptation has overtaken you except such as is common to man; but God is faithful, who will not allow you to be tempted beyond what you are able, but with the temptation will also make the way of escape, that you may be able to bear it. 1 CORINTHIANS 10:13

Wait on the Lord; be of good courage, and He shall strengthen your heart; wait, I say, on the Lord! PSALM 27:14

For You, O Lord, will bless the righteous; with favor You will surround him as with a shield. PSALM 5:12

For the Lord loves justice, and does not forsake His saints; they are preserved forever, but the descendants of the wicked shall be cut off. PSALM 37:28

"The hand of our God is upon all those for good who seek Him, but His power and His wrath are against all those who forsake Him."

EZRA 8:22

So the ransomed of the Lord shall return, and come to Zion with singing, with everlasting joy on their heads; they shall obtain joy and gladness, and sorrow and sighing shall flee away. ISAIAH 51:11

And He said to me, "My grace is sufficient for you, for My strength is made perfect in weakness." Therefore most gladly I will rather boast in my infirmities, that the power of Christ may rest upon me. 2 CORINTHIANS 12:9

For in that He Himself has suffered, being tempted, He is able to aid those who are tempted. HEBREWS 2:18

You are of God, little children, and have overcome them, because He who is in you is greater than he who is in the world. 1 JOHN 4:4

Adoption

For as many as are led by the Spirit of God, these are sons of God.

For you did not receive the spirit of bondage again to fear, but you received the Spirit of adoption by whom we cry out, "Abba, Father." ROMANS 8:14–15

For you are all sons of God through faith in Christ Jesus. GALATIANS 3:26

Having predestined us to adoption as sons by Jesus Christ to Himself, according to the good pleasure of His will. EPHESIANS 1:5

Behold what manner of love the Father has bestowed on us, that we should be called children of God! Therefore the world does not know us, because it did not know Him.

Beloved, now we are children of God; and it has not yet been revealed what we shall be, but we know that when He is revealed, we shall be like Him, for we shall see Him as He is.

1 JOHN 3:1–2

But as many as received Him, to them He gave the right to become children of God, even to those who believe in His name. JOHN 1:12

"And it shall come to pass in the place where it was said to them, 'You are not My people,' there they will be called sons of the living God." ROMANS 9:26

But when the fullness of the time had come, God sent forth His Son, born of a woman, born under the law, to redeem those who were under the law, that we might receive the adoption as sons.

GALATIANS 4:4–5

That at that time you were without Christ, being aliens from the commonwealth of Israel and strangers from the covenants of promise, having no hope and without God in the world.

But now in Christ Jesus you who once were far off have been made near by the blood of Christ. EPHESIANS 2:12–13

Now, therefore, you are no longer strangers and foreigners, but fellow citizens with the saints and members of the household of God,

in whom you also are being built together for a habitation of God in the Spirit.

EPHESIANS 2:19,22

And because you are sons, God has sent forth the Spirit of His Son into your hearts, crying out, "Abba, Father!"

Therefore you are no longer a slave but a son, and if a son, then an heir of God through Christ. GALATIANS 4:6–7

"I will be a Father to you, and you shall be My sons and daughters, says the Lord Almighty." 2 CORINTHIANS 6:18

Doubtless You are our Father, though Abraham was ignorant of us, and Israel does not acknowledge us. You, O Lord, are our Father; our Redeemer from Everlasting is Your name. ISAIAH 63:16

"For whoever does the will of My Father in heaven is My brother and sister and mother."

MATTHEW 12:50

For both He who sanctifies and those who are being sanctified are all of one, for which reason He is not ashamed to call them brethren. HEBREWS 2:11

For whom He foreknew, He also predestined to be conformed to the image of His Son, that He might be the firstborn among many brethren. ROMANS 8:29

"For whom the Lord loves He chastens, and scourges every son whom He receives."

If you endure chastening, God deals with

you as with sons; for what son is there whom a father does not chasten? HEBREWS 12:6–7

Perseverance

And we desire that each one of you show the same diligence to the full assurance of hope until the end,

that you do not become sluggish, but imitate those who through faith and patience inherit the promises. HEBREWS 6:11–12

For whatever is born of God overcomes the world. And this is the victory that has overcome the world—our faith.

Who is he who overcomes the world, but he who believes that Jesus is the Son of God?

1 JOHN 5:4–5

For he who lacks these things is shortsighted, even to blindness, and has forgotten that he was purged from his old sins.

Therefore, brethren, be even more diligent to make your calling and election sure, for if you do these things you will never stumble.

2 PETER 1:9–10

Therefore do not cast away your confidence, which has great reward.

For you have need of endurance, so that after you have done the will of God, you may receive the promise. HEBREWS 10:35–36

In the body of His flesh through death, to present you holy, and blameless, and irreproachable in His sight—

if indeed you continue in the faith, grounded and steadfast, and are not moved away from the hope of the gospel which you heard, which was preached to every creature under heaven, of which I, Paul, became a minister.

COLOSSIANS 1:22–23

"He who overcomes shall be clothed in white garments, and I will not blot out his name from the Book of Life; but I will confess his name before My Father and before His angels."

REVELATION 3:5

As you have therefore received Christ Jesus the Lord, so walk in Him,

rooted and built up in Him and established in the faith, as you have been taught, abounding in it with thanksgiving. COLOSSIANS 2:6–7

Let us hold fast the confession of our hope without wavering, for He who promised is faithful.

And let us consider one another in order to stir up love and good works. HEBREWS 10:23–24

And the Lord said, "Simon, Simon! Indeed, Satan has asked for you, that he may sift you as wheat.

"But I have prayed for you, that your faith should not fail; and when you have returned to Me, strengthen your brethren." LUKE 22:31–32

"I do not pray that You should take them out of the world, but that You should keep them from the evil one." JOHN 17:15

Therefore submit to God. Resist the devil and he will flee from you. JAMES 4:7

Then the Lord knows how to deliver the godly out of temptations and to reserve the unjust under punishment for the day of judgment. 2 PETER 2:9

For if we sin willfully after we have received the knowledge of the truth, there no longer remains a sacrifice for sins, but a certain fearful expectation of judgment, and fiery indignation which will devour the adversaries. HEBREWS 10:26–27

He gives power to the weak, and to those who have no might He increases strength.

Even the youths shall faint and be weary, and the young men shall utterly fall,

but those who wait on the Lord shall renew their strength; they shall mount up with wings like eagles, they shall run and not be weary, they shall walk and not faint. ISAIAH 40:29–31

For God has not given us a spirit of fear, but of power and of love and of a sound mind. 2 TIMOTHY 1:7

Be of good courage, and He shall strengthen your heart, all you who hope in the Lord. PSALM 31:24

"So I will strengthen them in the Lord, and they shall walk up and down in His name," says the Lord. ZECHARIAH 10:12

Strengthen the weak hands, and make firm the feeble knees.

Say to those who are fearful-hearted, "Be strong, do not fear! Behold, your God will come with vengeance, with the recompense of God; He will come and save you." ISAIAH 35:3–4

"In that day the Lord will defend the inhabitants of Jerusalem; the one who is feeble among them in that day shall be like David, and the house of David shall be like God, like the Angel of the Lord before them." ZECHARIAH 12:8

Guidance

"However, when He, the Spirit of truth, has come, He will guide you into all truth; for He will not speak on His own authority, but whatever He hears He will speak; and He will tell you things to come." JOHN 16:13

The steps of a good man are ordered by the Lord, and He delights in his way. PSALM 37:23

Brethren, I write no new commandment to you, but an old commandment which you have had from the beginning. The old commandment is the word which you heard from the beginning. 1 JOHN 2:7

"And I will pray the Father, and He will give you another Helper, that He may abide with you forever.

"I will not leave you orphans; I will come to you." JOHN 14:16,18

For He shall give His angels charge over you, to keep you in all your ways.

They shall bear you up in their hands, lest you dash your foot against a stone.

PSALM 91:11–12

I say then: Walk in the Spirit, and you shall not fulfill the lust of the flesh. GALATIANS 5:16

I have seen his ways, and will heal him; I will also lead him, and restore comforts to him and to his mourners. ISAIAH 57:18

For this is God, our God forever and ever; He will be our guide even to death. PSALM 48:14

You will guide me with Your counsel, and afterward receive me to glory. PSALM 73:24

In all your ways acknowledge Him, and He shall direct your paths. PROVERBS 3:6

For He instructs him in right judgment, his God teaches him. ISAIAH 28:26

I will bring the blind by a way they did not know; I will lead them in paths they have not known. I will make darkness light before them, and crooked places straight. These things I will do for them, and not forsake them. ISAIAH 42:16

A man's heart plans his way, but the Lord directs his steps. PROVERBS 16:9

"Indeed He would have brought you out of dire distress, into a broad place where there is no restraint; and what is set on your table would be full of richness." JOB 36:16

Then they cried out to the Lord in their trouble, and He saved them out of their distresses. PSALM 107:19

For a righteous man may fall seven times and rise again, but the wicked shall fall by calamity. PROVERBS 24:16

The righteous is delivered from trouble, and it comes to the wicked instead.

PROVERBS 11:8

PROMISES FOR SPIRITUAL GROWTH

In Faith and Trust

❧ For whatever is born of God overcomes the world. And this is the victory that has overcome the world—our faith. 1 JOHN 5:4

He Himself gave some to be apostles, some prophets, some evangelists, and some pastors and teachers,

for the equipping of the saints for the work of ministry, for the edifying of the body of Christ,

till we all come to the unity of the faith and the knowledge of the Son of God, to a perfect man, to the measure of the stature of the fullness of Christ. EPHESIANS 4:11–13

That the genuineness of your faith, being much more precious than gold that perishes, though it is tested by fire, may be found to praise, honor, and glory at the revelation of Jesus Christ,

whom having not seen you love. Though now you do not see Him, yet believing, you

rejoice with joy inexpressible and full of glory,
receiving the end of your faith—the salvation of your souls. 1 PETER 1:7–9

So then faith comes by hearing, and hearing by the word of God. ROMANS 10:17

Looking unto Jesus, the author and finisher of our faith, who for the joy that was set before Him endured the cross, despising the shame, and has sat down at the right hand of the throne of God. HEBREWS 12:2

"For the eyes of the Lord are on the righteous, and his ears are open to their prayers; but the face of the Lord is against those who do evil."

And who is he who will harm you if you become followers of what is good?

1 PETER 3:12–13

For in it the righteousness of God is revealed from faith to faith; as it is written, "The just shall live by faith." ROMANS 1:17

For we walk by faith, not by sight.

2 CORINTHIANS 5:7

But without faith it is impossible to please Him, for he who comes to God must believe that He is, and that He is a rewarder of those who diligently seek Him. HEBREWS 11:6

For I say, through the grace given to me, to everyone who is among you, not to think of himself more highly than he ought to think, but to think soberly, as God has dealt to each one a measure of faith. ROMANS 12:3

Now faith is the substance of things hoped for, the evidence of things not seen.
HEBREWS 11:1

"He will guard the feet of His saints, but the wicked shall be silent in darkness. For by strength no man shall prevail." 1 SAMUEL 2:9

Yet the righteous will hold to his way, and he who has clean hands will be stronger and stronger. JOB 17:9

Knowing that the testing of your faith produces patience. JAMES 1:3

Blessed is the man who endures temptation; for when he has been proved, he will receive the crown of life which the Lord has promised to those who love Him. JAMES 1:12

When you pass through the waters, I will be with you; and through the rivers, they shall not overflow you. When you walk through the fire, you shall not be burned, nor shall the flame scorch you. ISAIAH 43:2

"For the eyes of the Lord run to and fro throughout the whole earth, to show Himself strong on behalf of those whose heart is loyal to Him. In this you have done foolishly; therefore from now on you shall have wars."

2 CHRONICLES 16:9

But the Lord is faithful, who will establish you and guard you from the evil one.

2 THESSALONIANS 3:3

In Love of God

❧ And we know that all things work together for good to those who love God, to those who are the called according to His purpose.
ROMANS 8:28

The Lord preserves all who love Him, but all the wicked He will destroy. PSALM 145:20

"He who has My commandments and keeps them, it is he who loves Me. And he who loves Me will be loved by My Father, and I will love him and manifest Myself to him." JOHN 14:21

Listen, my beloved brethren: Has God not chosen the poor of this world to be rich in faith and heirs of the kingdom which He promised to those who love Him? JAMES 2:5

But as it is written: "Eye has not seen, nor ear heard, nor have entered into the heart of man the things which God has prepared for those who love Him." 1 CORINTHIANS 2:9

In this is love, not that we loved God, but that He loved us and sent His Son to be the propitiation for our sins.

And we have known and believed the love that God has for us. God is love, and he who abides in love abides in God, and God in him.

We love Him because He first loved us.

1 JOHN 4:10,16,19

But if anyone loves God, this one is known by Him. 1 CORINTHIANS 8:3

Blessed is the man who endures temptation; for when he has been proved, he will receive the crown of life which the Lord has promised to those who love Him. JAMES 1:12

But showing mercy to thousands, to those who love Me and keep My commandments.

EXODUS 20:6

And I said: "I pray, Lord God of heaven, O great and awesome God, You who keep Your covenant and mercy with those who love You and observe Your commandments."

NEHEMIAH 1:5

"Therefore know that the Lord your God, He is God, the faithful God who keeps covenant and mercy for a thousand generations with those who love Him and keep His commandments." DEUTERONOMY 7:9

"Thus let all Your enemies perish, O Lord! But let those who love Him be like the sun when it comes out in full strength." So the land had rest for forty years. JUDGES 5:31

"If you keep My commandments, you will abide in My love, just as I have kept My Father's commandments and abide in His love.

"You are My friends if you do whatever I command you." JOHN 15:10,14

"And you shall love the LORD your God with all your heart, with all your soul, with all your mind, and with all your strength." This is the first commandment.

"And to love Him with all the heart, with all the understanding, with all the soul, and with all the strength, and to love one's neighbor as oneself, is more than all the whole burnt offerings and sacrifices." MARK 12:30,33

"For the Father Himself loves you, because you have loved Me, and have believed that I came forth from God." JOHN 16:27

In Love of Others

Beloved, if God so loved us, we also ought to love one another.

No one has seen God at any time. If we love one another, God abides in us, and His love has been perfected in us. 1 JOHN 4:11–12

Finally, all of you be of one mind, having compassion for one another; love as brothers, be tenderhearted, be courteous;

not returning evil for evil or reviling for reviling, but on the contrary blessing, knowing that you were called to this, that you may inherit a blessing. 1 PETER 3:8–9

"This is My commandment, that you love one another as I have loved you.

"Greater love has no one than this, than to lay down one's life for his friends." JOHN 15:12–13

"'And you shall love the Lord your God with all your heart, with all your soul, with all your mind, and with all your strength.' This is the first commandment.

"And the second, like it, is this: 'You shall love your neighbor as yourself.' There is no other commandment greater than these."

MARK 12:30–31

Though I speak with the tongues of men and of angels, but have not love, I have become as sounding brass or a clanging cymbal.

And though I have the gift of prophecy, and understand all mysteries and all knowledge, and though I have all faith, so that I could remove mountains, but have not love, I am nothing.

And though I bestow all my goods to feed the poor, and though I give my body to be burned, but have not love, it profits me nothing.

Love suffers long and is kind; love does not envy; love does not parade itself, is not puffed up;

does not behave rudely, does not seek its own, is not provoked, thinks no evil;

does not rejoice in iniquity, but rejoices in the truth;

bears all things, believes all things, hopes all things, endures all things.

Love never fails. But whether there are prophecies, they will fail; whether there are tongues, they will cease; whether there is knowledge, it will vanish away.

1 CORINTHIANS 13:1–8

"By this all will know that you are My disciples, if you have love for one another."

JOHN 13:35

"But I say to you, love your enemies, bless those who curse you, do good to those who hate you, and pray for those who spitefully use you and persecute you." MATTHEW 5:44

And this commandment we have from Him: that he who loves God must love his brother also. 1 JOHN 4:21

Beloved, do not avenge yourselves, but rather give place to wrath; for it is written, "Vengeance is Mine, I will repay," says the Lord.

"Therefore if your enemy hungers, feed him; if he thirsts, give him a drink; for in so doing you will heap coals of fire on his head."

Do not be overcome by evil, but overcome evil with good. ROMANS 12:19–21

Since you have purified your souls in obeying the truth through the Spirit in sincere love of the brethren, love one another fervently with a pure heart. 1 PETER 1:22

Love does no harm to a neighbor; therefore love is the fulfillment of the law. ROMANS 13:10

Beloved, let us love one another, for love is of God; and everyone who loves is born of God and knows God.

He who does not love does not know God, for God is love. 1 JOHN 4:7–8

He who loves his brother abides in the light, and there is no cause for stumbling in him.

1 JOHN 2:10

But do not forget to do good and to share, for with such sacrifices God is well pleased.

HEBREWS 13:16

Behold, how good and how pleasant it is for brethren to dwell together in unity!

It is like the precious oil upon the head, running down on the beard, the beard of Aaron, running down on the edge of his garments.

PSALM 133:1–2

We know that we have passed from death to life, because we love the brethren. He who does not love his brother abides in death.

My little children, let us not love in word or in tongue, but in deed and in truth.

And by this we know that we are of the truth, and shall assure our hearts before Him.

1 JOHN 3:14,18–19

For God is not unjust to forget your work and labor of love which you have shown toward His name, in that you have ministered to the saints, and do minister. HEBREWS 6:10

Finally, brethren, farewell. Become complete. Be of good comfort, be of one mind, live in peace; and the God of love and peace will be with you. 2 CORINTHIANS 13:11

In Peace

❧ Be anxious for nothing, but in everything by prayer and supplication, with thanksgiving, let your requests be made known to God;

and the peace of God, which surpasses all understanding, will guard your hearts and minds through Christ Jesus. PHILIPPIANS 4:6–7

Therefore, having been justified by faith, we have peace with God through our Lord Jesus Christ. ROMANS 5:1

"Peace I leave with you, My peace I give to you; not as the world gives do I give to you. Let not your heart be troubled, neither let it be afraid." JOHN 14:27

For to be carnally minded is death, but to be spiritually minded is life and peace.
ROMANS 8:6

You will keep him in perfect peace, whose mind is stayed on You, because he trusts in You.
ISAIAH 26:3

Great peace have those who love Your law, and nothing causes them to stumble.

PSALM 119:165

Finally, brethren, farewell. Become complete. Be of good comfort, be of one mind, live in peace; and the God of love and peace will be with you. 2 CORINTHIANS 13:11

Lord, You will establish peace for us, for You have also done all our works in us.

ISAIAH 26:12

Mark the blameless man, and observe the upright; for the future of that man is peace.

PSALM 37:37

"For you shall go out with joy, and be led out with peace; the mountains and the hills shall break forth into singing before you, and all the trees of the field shall clap their hands."

ISAIAH 55:12

For the kingdom of God is not food and drink, but righteousness and peace and joy in the Holy Spirit.

For he who serves Christ in these things is

acceptable to God and approved by men.

Therefore let us pursue the things which make for peace and the things by which one may edify another. ROMANS 14:17–19

The work of righteousness will be peace, and the effect of righteousness, quietness and assurance forever. ISAIAH 32:17

Now may the Lord of peace Himself give you peace always in every way. The Lord be with you all. 2 THESSALONIANS 3:16

I will hear what God the Lord will speak, for He will speak peace to His people and to His saints; but let them not turn back to folly.

PSALM 85:8

And let the peace of God rule in your hearts, to which also you were called in one body; and be thankful. COLOSSIANS 3:15

Now may the God of hope fill you with all joy and peace in believing, that you may abound in hope by the power of the Holy Spirit.

ROMANS 15:13

All your children shall be taught by the Lord, and great shall be the peace of your children. ISAIAH 54:13

But now in Christ Jesus you who once were far off have been made near by the blood of Christ.

For He Himself is our peace, who has made both one, and has broken down the middle wall of division between us.

EPHESIANS 2:13–14

In Maturity

If any of you lacks wisdom, let him ask of God, who gives to all liberally and without reproach, and it will be given to him. JAMES 1:5

Grow in the grace and knowledge of our Lord and Savior Jesus Christ. To Him be the glory both now and forever. Amen. 2 PETER 3:18

For though by this time you ought to be teachers, you need someone to teach you again the first principles of the oracles of God; and you have come to need milk and not solid food.

Therefore, leaving the discussion of the elementary principles of Christ, let us go on to perfection, not laying again the foundation of repentance from dead works and of faith toward God,

of the doctrine of baptisms, of laying on of hands, of resurrection of the dead, and of eternal judgment. HEBREWS 5:12; 6:1–2

"However, when He, the Spirit of truth, has come, He will guide you into all truth; for He will not speak on His own authority, but whatever He hears He will speak; and He will tell you things to come." JOHN 16:13

If you seek her as silver, and search for her as for hidden treasures;

Then you will understand the fear of the Lord, and find the knowledge of God.

For the Lord gives wisdom; from His mouth come knowledge and understanding;

He stores up sound wisdom for the upright; He is a shield to those who walk uprightly.

PROVERBS 2:4–7

Now we have received, not the spirit of the world, but the Spirit who is from God, that we might know the things that have been freely given to us by God. 1 CORINTHIANS 2:12

Evil men do not understand justice, but those who seek the Lord understand all.

PROVERBS 28:5

But of Him you are in Christ Jesus, who became for us wisdom from God—and righteousness and sanctification and redemption. 1 CORINTHIANS 1:30

"For I will give you a mouth and wisdom which all your adversaries will not be able to contradict or resist." LUKE 21:15

Being confident of this very thing, that He who has begun a good work in you will complete it until the day of Jesus Christ.

PHILIPPIANS 1:6

Now may the God of peace Himself sanctify you completely; and may your whole spirit, soul, and body be preserved blameless at the coming of our Lord Jesus Christ.

He who calls you is faithful, who also will do it. 1 THESSALONIANS 5:23–24

Then Jesus spoke to them again, saying, "I am the light of the world. He who follows Me shall not walk in darkness, but have the light of life." JOHN 8:12

The fear of the Lord is the beginning of wisdom; a good understanding have all those who do His commandments. His praise endures forever. PSALM 111:10

I will bring the blind by a way they did not know; I will lead them in paths they have not known. I will make darkness light before them, and crooked places straight. These things I will do for them, and not forsake them. ISAIAH 42:16

"With Him are wisdom and strength, He has counsel and understanding." JOB 12:13

I will instruct you and teach you in the way you should go; I will guide you with My eye.
PSALM 32:8

I say then: Walk in the Spirit, and you shall not fulfill the lust of the flesh. GALATIANS 5:16

For if these things are yours and abound, you will be neither barren nor unfruitful in the knowledge of our Lord Jesus Christ. 2 PETER 1:8

He shall be like a tree planted by the rivers of water, that brings forth its fruit in its season, whose leaf also shall not wither; and whatever he does shall prosper. PSALM 1:3

"Every branch in Me that does not bear fruit He takes away; and every branch that bears fruit He prunes, that it may bear more fruit.

"I am the vine, you are the branches. He who abides in Me, and I in him, bears much fruit; for without Me you can do nothing." JOHN 15:2,5

In Forgiving Others

❧ "And whenever you stand praying, if you have anything against anyone, forgive him, that your Father in heaven may also forgive you your trespasses." MARK 11:25

Then Peter came to Him and said, "Lord, how often shall my brother sin against me, and I forgive him? Up to seven times?"

Jesus said to him, "I do not say to you, up to seven times, but up to seventy times seven."

MATTHEW 18:21–22

Bearing with one another, and forgiving one another, if anyone has a complaint against another; even as Christ forgave you, so you also must do. COLOSSIANS 3:13

"For if you forgive men their trespasses, your heavenly Father will also forgive you.

"But if you do not forgive men their trespasses, neither will your Father forgive your trespasses." MATTHEW 6:14–15

"Therefore if your enemy hungers, feed him; if he thirsts, give him a drink; for in so doing you will heap coals of fire on his head."

Do not be overcome by evil, but overcome evil with good. ROMANS 12:20–21

"But I say to you, love your enemies, bless those who curse you, do good to those who hate you, and pray for those who spitefully use you and persecute you,

"that you may be sons of your Father in heaven; for He makes His sun rise on the evil and on the good, and sends rain on the just and on the unjust." MATTHEW 5:44–45

For this is commendable, if because of conscience toward God one endures grief, suffering wrongfully.

For what credit is it if, when you are beaten for your faults, you take it patiently? But when you do good and suffer for it, if you take it patiently, this is commendable before God.

For to this you were called, because Christ also suffered for us, leaving us an example, that you should follow His steps:

"Who committed no sin, nor was guile found in His mouth";

who, when He was reviled, did not revile in return; when He suffered, He did not threaten, but committed Himself to Him who judges righteously. 1 PETER 2:19–23

Do not say, "I will recompense evil"; wait for the Lord, and He will save you. PROVERBS 20:22

"But love your enemies, do good, and lend, hoping for nothing in return; and your reward will be great, and you will be sons of the Highest. For He is kind to the unthankful and evil.

"Judge not, and you shall not be judged. Condemn not, and you shall not be condemned. Forgive, and you will be forgiven." LUKE 6:35,37

"Blessed are those who are persecuted for righteousness' sake, for theirs is the kingdom of heaven.

"Blessed are you when they revile and persecute you, and say all kinds of evil against you falsely for My sake.

"Rejoice and be exceedingly glad, for great is your reward in heaven, for so they persecuted the prophets who were before you."

MATTHEW 5:10–12

For we know Him who said, "Vengeance is Mine; I will repay, says the Lord." And again, "The Lord will judge His people." HEBREWS 10:30

Let all bitterness, wrath, anger, clamor, and evil speaking be put away from you, with all malice.

And be kind to one another, tenderhearted, forgiving one another, just as God in Christ also forgave you. EPHESIANS 4:31–32

If you are reproached for the name of Christ, blessed are you, for the Spirit of glory and of God rests upon you. On their part He is blasphemed, but on your part He is glorified.

1 PETER 4:14

In Fellowship

❧ "A new commandment I give to you, that you love one another; as I have loved you, that you also love one another.

"By this all will know that you are My disciples, if you have love for one another."

JOHN 13:34–35

Let the word of Christ dwell in you richly in all wisdom, teaching and admonishing one another in psalms and hymns and spiritual songs, singing with grace in your hearts to the Lord. COLOSSIANS 3:16

And they continued steadfastly in the apostles' doctrine and fellowship, in the breaking of bread, and in prayers.

So continuing daily with one accord in the temple, and breaking bread from house to house, they ate their food with gladness and simplicity of heart,

praising God and having favor with all the people. And the Lord added to the church daily those who were being saved. ACTS 2:42,46–47

That which we have seen and heard we declare to you, that you also may have fellowship with us; and truly our fellowship is with the Father and with His Son Jesus Christ.

But if we walk in the light as He is in the light, we have fellowship with one another, and the blood of Jesus Christ His Son cleanses us from all sin. 1 JOHN 1:3,7

Then those who feared the Lord spoke to one another, and the Lord listened and heard them; so a book of remembrance was written before Him for those who fear the Lord and who meditate on His name. MALACHI 3:16

That their hearts may be encouraged, being knit together in love, and attaining to all riches of the full assurance of understanding, to the knowledge of the mystery of God, both of the Father and of Christ. COLOSSIANS 2:2

And walk in love, as Christ also has loved us and given Himself for us, an offering and a sacrifice to God for a sweet-smelling aroma.
EPHESIANS 5:2

We took sweet counsel together, and walked to the house of God in the throng.
PSALM 55:14

"That they all may be one, as You, Father, are in Me, and I in You; that they also may be one in Us, that the world may believe that You sent Me.

"And the glory which You gave Me I have given them, that they may be one just as We are one:

"I in them, and You in Me; that they may be made perfect in one, and that the world may know that You have sent Me, and have loved them as You have loved Me." JOHN 17:21–23

As iron sharpens iron, so a man sharpens the countenance of his friend. PROVERBS 27:17

God is faithful, by whom you were called into the fellowship of His Son, Jesus Christ our Lord. 1 CORINTHIANS 1:9

Two are better than one, because they have a good reward for their labor.

For if they fall, one will lift up his companion. But woe to him who is alone when he falls, for he has no one to help him up.

ECCLESIASTES 4:9–10

Let each of us please his neighbor for his good, leading to edification.

May the God of patience and comfort grant you to be like-minded toward one another, according to Christ Jesus. ROMANS 15:2,5

"I have shown you in every way, by laboring like this, that you must support the weak. And remember the words of the Lord Jesus, that He said, 'It is more blessed to give than to receive.'"

ACTS 20:35

A man who has friends must himself be friendly, but there is a friend who sticks closer than a brother. PROVERBS 18:24

"He who receives you receives Me, and he who receives Me receives Him who sent Me.
"He who receives a prophet in the name of a prophet shall receive a prophet's reward. And he who receives a righteous man in the name of a righteous man shall receive a righteous man's reward." MATTHEW 10:40–41

In Holiness

❧ Blessed are the pure in heart, for they shall see God. MATTHEW 5:8

To the pure all things are pure, but to those who are defiled and unbelieving nothing is pure; but even their mind and conscience are defiled.
TITUS 1:15

Who may ascend into the hill of the Lord? Or who may stand in His holy place?
He who has clean hands and a pure heart, who has not lifted up his soul to an idol, nor sworn deceitfully. PSALM 24:3–4

Therefore if anyone cleanses himself from the latter, he will be a vessel for honor, sanctified and useful for the Master, prepared for every good work. 2 TIMOTHY 2:21

A highway shall be there, and a road, and it shall be called the Highway of Holiness. The unclean shall not pass over it, but it shall be for others. Whoever walks the road, although a fool, shall not go astray. ISAIAH 35:8

Who gave Himself for us, that He might redeem us from every lawless deed and purify for Himself His own special people, zealous for good works. TITUS 2:14

But you were washed, but you were sanctified, but you were justified in the name of the Lord Jesus and by the Spirit of our God.
1 CORINTHIANS 6:11

To grant us that we, being delivered from the hand of our enemies, might serve Him without fear,
in holiness and righteousness before Him all the days of our life. LUKE 1:74–75

And you, who once were alienated and enemies in your mind by wicked works, yet now He has reconciled

in the body of His flesh through death, to present you holy, and blameless, and irreproachable in His sight. COLOSSIANS 1:21–22

"For their sakes I sanctify Myself, that they also may be sanctified by the truth." JOHN 17:19

Now may the God of peace Himself sanctify you completely; and may your whole spirit, soul, and body be preserved blameless at the coming of our Lord Jesus Christ.

1 THESSALONIANS 5:23

But we are bound to give thanks to God always for you, brethren beloved by the Lord, because God from the beginning chose you for salvation through sanctification by the Spirit and belief in the truth. 2 THESSALONIANS 2:13

"Then I will give them one heart, and I will put a new spirit within them, and take the stony heart out of their flesh, and give them a heart of flesh,

"that they may walk in My statutes and

keep My judgments and do them; and they shall be My people, and I will be their God."

EZEKIEL 11:19–20

But of Him you are in Christ Jesus, who became for us wisdom from God—and righteousness and sanctification and redemption. 1 CORINTHIANS 1:30

With the pure You will show Yourself pure; and with the devious You will show Yourself shrewd. PSALM 18:26

And if Christ is in you, the body is dead because of sin, but the Spirit is life because of righteousness. ROMANS 8:10

In Victory Over Sin

❧ Then the Lord knows how to deliver the godly out of temptations and to reserve the unjust under punishment for the day of judgment. 2 PETER 2:9

For sin shall not have dominion over you, for you are not under law but under grace.

ROMANS 6:14

Therefore let him who thinks he stands take heed lest he fall.

No temptation has overtaken you except such as is common to man; but God is faithful, who will not allow you to be tempted beyond what you are able, but with the temptation will also make the way of escape, that you may be able to bear it. 1 CORINTHIANS 10:12–13

For in that He Himself has suffered, being tempted, He is able to aid those who are tempted. HEBREWS 2:18

Be sober, be vigilant; because your adversary the devil walks about like a roaring lion, seeking whom he may devour.

Resist him, steadfast in the faith, knowing that the same sufferings are experienced by your brotherhood in the world. 1 PETER 5:8–9

Finally, my brethren, be strong in the Lord and in the power of His might.

Put on the whole armor of God, that you may be able to stand against the wiles of the devil.

Above all, taking the shield of faith with which you will be able to quench all the fiery darts of the wicked one. EPHESIANS 6:10–11,16

You are of God, little children, and have overcome them, because He who is in you is greater than he who is in the world. 1 JOHN 4:4

Your word I have hidden in my heart, that I might not sin against You. PSALM 119:11

He who covers his sins will not prosper, but whoever confesses and forsakes them will have mercy. PROVERBS 28:13

Blessed is the man who endures temptation; for when he has been proved, he will receive the crown of life which the Lord has promised to those who love Him.

Let no one say when he is tempted, "I am tempted by God"; for God cannot be tempted by evil, nor does He Himself tempt anyone.

But each one is tempted when he is drawn away by his own desires and enticed.

JAMES 1:12–14

If we confess our sins, He is faithful and just to forgive us our sins and to cleanse us from all unrighteousness. 1 JOHN 1:9

Therefore submit to God. Resist the devil and he will flee from you. JAMES 4:7

Seeing then that we have a great High Priest who has passed through the heavens, Jesus the Son of God, let us hold fast our confession.

For we do not have a High Priest who cannot sympathize with our weaknesses, but was in all points tempted as we are, yet without sin.

Let us therefore come boldly to the throne of grace, that we may obtain mercy and find grace to help in time of need. HEBREWS 4:14–16

In this you greatly rejoice, though now for a little while, if need be, you have been grieved by various trials,

that the genuineness of your faith, being much more precious than gold that perishes, though it is tested by fire, may be found to praise, honor, and glory at the revelation of Jesus Christ. 1 PETER 1:6–7

O wretched man that I am! Who will deliver me from this body of death?

I thank God—through Jesus Christ our Lord! So then, with the mind I myself serve the law of God, but with the flesh the law of sin.

ROMANS 7:24–25

I say then: Walk in the Spirit, and you shall not fulfill the lust of the flesh. GALATIANS 5:16

Yet in all these things we are more than conquerors through Him who loved us.

ROMANS 8:37

It is good that you grasp this, and also not remove your hand from the other; for he who fears God will escape them all. ECCLESIASTES 7:18

For the law of the Spirit of life in Christ Jesus has made me free from the law of sin and death.

For what the law could not do in that it was weak through the flesh, God did by sending His own Son in the likeness of sinful flesh, on account of sin: He condemned sin in the flesh,

that the righteous requirement of the law might be fulfilled in us who do not walk according to the flesh but according to the Spirit. ROMANS 8:2–4

In Finding His Will

❧ I will instruct you and teach you in the way you should go; I will guide you with My eye.
PSALM 32:8

And we know that the Son of God has come and has given us an understanding, that we may know Him who is true; and we are in Him who is true, in His Son Jesus Christ. This is the true God and eternal life. 1 JOHN 5:20

"If anyone wants to do His will, he shall know concerning the doctrine, whether it is from God or whether I speak on My own authority." JOHN 7:17

Trust in the Lord with all your heart, and lean not on your own understanding;
in all your ways acknowledge Him, and He shall direct your paths. PROVERBS 3:5–6

"For I will give you a mouth and wisdom which all your adversaries will not be able to contradict or resist." LUKE 21:15

"However, when He, the Spirit of truth, has come, He will guide you into all truth; for He will not speak on His own authority, but whatever He hears He will speak; and He will tell you things to come." JOHN 16:13

Evil men do not understand justice, but those who seek the Lord understand all.
PROVERBS 28:5

Many people shall come and say, "Come, and let us go up to the mountain of the Lord, to the house of the God of Jacob; He will teach us His ways, and we shall walk in His paths." For out of Zion shall go forth the law, and the word of the Lord from Jerusalem. ISAIAH 2:3

Turn at my reproof; surely I will pour out my spirit on you; I will make my words known to you. PROVERBS 1:23

The entrance of Your words gives light; it gives understanding to the simple. PSALM 119:130

Commit your works to the Lord, and your thoughts will be established. PROVERBS 16:3

I will bring the blind by a way they did not know; I will lead them in paths they have not known. I will make darkness light before them, and crooked places straight. These things I will do for them, and not forsake them. ISAIAH 42:16

Let us know, let us pursue the knowledge of the Lord. His going forth is established as the morning; He will come to us like the rain, like the latter and former rain to the earth.

HOSEA 6:3

For God gives wisdom and knowledge and joy to a man who is good in His sight; but to the sinner He gives the work of gathering and collecting, that he may give to him who is good before God. ECCLESIASTES 2:26

My soul, wait silently for God alone, for my expectation is from Him. PSALM 62:5

"With Him are wisdom and strength, He has counsel and understanding." JOB 12:13

The Lord will perfect that which concerns me; Your mercy, O Lord, endures forever; do not forsake the works of Your hands.

PSALM 138:8

If any of you lacks wisdom, let him ask of God, who gives to all liberally and without reproach, and it will be given to him. JAMES 1:5

Cast your burden on the Lord, and He shall sustain you; He shall never permit the righteous to be moved. PSALM 55:22

If you seek her as silver, and search for her as for hidden treasures;

Then you will understand the fear of the Lord, and find the knowledge of God.

For the Lord gives wisdom; from His mouth come knowledge and understanding;

He stores up sound wisdom for the upright; He is a shield to those who walk uprightly.

PROVERBS 2:4–7

For it is the God who commanded light to shine out of darkness who has shone in our hearts to give the light of the knowledge of the glory of God in the face of Jesus Christ.

2 CORINTHIANS 4:6

At that time Jesus answered and said, "I thank You, Father, Lord of heaven and earth, because You have hidden these things from the wise and prudent and have revealed them to babes." MATTHEW 11:25

But the natural man does not receive the things of the Spirit of God, for they are foolishness to him; nor can he know them, because they are spiritually discerned.

But he who is spiritual judges all things, yet he himself is rightly judged by no one.

1 CORINTHIANS 2:14–15

In Security

❧ You are of God, little children, and have overcome them, because He who is in you is greater than he who is in the world. 1 JOHN 4:4

"My Father, who has given them to Me, is greater than all; and no one is able to snatch them out of My Father's hand." JOHN 10:29

Now to Him who is able to keep you from stumbling, and to present you faultless before the presence of His glory with exceeding joy,

to God our Savior, who alone is wise, be glory and majesty, dominion and power, both now and forever. Amen. JUDE 24–25

Yet in all these things we are more than conquerors through Him who loved us.

For I am persuaded that neither death nor life, angels nor principalities nor powers, nor things present nor things to come,

nor height nor depth, nor any other created thing, shall be able to separate us from the love of God which is in Christ Jesus our Lord.

ROMANS 8:37–39

Why are you cast down, O my soul? And why are you disquieted within me? Hope in God, for I shall yet praise Him for the help of His countenance. PSALM 42:5

And it will be said in that day: "Behold, this is our God; we have waited for Him, and He will save us. This is the Lord; we have waited for Him; we will be glad and rejoice in His salvation." ISAIAH 25:9

Surely goodness and mercy shall follow me all the days of my life; and I will dwell in the house of the Lord forever. PSALM 23:6

And who is he who will harm you if you become followers of what is good? 1 PETER 3:13

Lift up your eyes on high, and see who has created these things, who brings out their host by number; He calls them all by name, by the greatness of His might and the strength of His power; not one is missing. ISAIAH 40:26

Being confident of this very thing, that He who has begun a good work in you will complete it until the day of Jesus Christ.
PHILIPPIANS 1:6

Therefore do not cast away your confidence, which has great reward.

For you have need of endurance, so that after you have done the will of God, you may receive the promise. HEBREWS 10:35–36

I can do all things through Christ who strengthens me. PHILIPPIANS 4:13

So we may boldly say: "The Lord is my helper; I will not fear. What can man do to me?"
HEBREWS 13:6

The Lord God is my strength; He will make my feet like deer's feet, and He will make me walk on my high hills. HABAKKUK 3:19

Now this is the confidence that we have in Him, that if we ask anything according to His will, He hears us.

And if we know that He hears us, whatever we ask, we know that we have the petitions that we have asked of Him. 1 JOHN 5:14–15

We know that whoever is born of God does not sin; but he who has been born of God keeps himself, and the wicked one does not touch him. 1 JOHN 5:18

When you pass through the waters, I will be with you; and through the rivers, they shall not overflow you. When you walk through the fire, you shall not be burned, nor shall the flame scorch you. ISAIAH 43:2

If I say, "My foot slips," Your mercy, O Lord, will hold me up. PSALM 94:18

Therefore, brethren, be even more diligent to make your calling and election sure, for if you do these things you will never stumble.

2 PETER 1:10

In Answered Prayer

"And whatever you ask in My name, that I will do, that the Father may be glorified in the Son.

"If you ask anything in My name, I will do it." JOHN 14:13–14

And whatever we ask we receive from Him, because we keep His commandments and do those things that are pleasing in His sight.

1 JOHN 3:22

"And all things, whatever you ask in prayer, believing, you will receive." MATTHEW 21:22

"If you abide in Me, and My words abide in you, you will ask what you desire, and it shall be done for you." JOHN 15:7

And the prayer of faith will save the sick, and the Lord will raise him up. And if he has committed sins, he will be forgiven.

Confess your trespasses to one another, and pray for one another, that you may be healed. The effective, fervent prayer of a righteous man avails much. JAMES 5:15–16

"And in that day you will ask Me nothing. Most assuredly, I say to you, whatever you ask the Father in My name He will give you.

"Until now you have asked nothing in My name. Ask, and you will receive, that your joy may be full." JOHN 16:23–24

Now this is the confidence that we have in Him, that if we ask anything according to His will, He hears us.

And if we know that He hears us, whatever we ask, we know that we have the petitions that we have asked of Him.

If anyone sees his brother sinning a sin which does not lead to death, he will ask, and He will give him life for those who commit sin not leading to death. There is sin leading to death. I do not say that he should pray about that. 1 JOHN 5:14–16

I will bring the one third through the fire, will refine them as silver is refined, and test them as gold is tested. They will call on My name, and I will answer them. I will say, "This is

My people"; and each one will say, "The Lord is my God." ZECHARIAH 13:9

But know that the Lord has set apart for Himself him who is godly; the Lord will hear when I call to Him. PSALM 4:3

The eyes of the Lord are on the righteous, and His ears are open to their cry.

The righteous cry out, and the Lord hears, and delivers them out of all their troubles.

PSALM 34:15,17

The Lord is far from the wicked, but He hears the prayer of the righteous. PROVERBS 15:29

He shall call upon Me, and I will answer him; I will be with him in trouble; I will deliver him and honor him. PSALM 91:15

"It shall come to pass that before they call, I will answer; and while they are still speaking, I will hear." ISAIAH 65:24

O You who hear prayer, to You all flesh will come. PSALM 65:2

Then you will call upon Me and go and pray to Me, and I will listen to you.

JEREMIAH 29:12

"Ask, and it will be given to you; seek, and you will find; knock, and it will be opened to you.

"For everyone who asks receives, and he who seeks finds, and to him who knocks it will be opened.

"If you then, being evil, know how to give good gifts to your children, how much more will your Father who is in heaven give good things to those who ask Him!" MATTHEW 7:7–8,11

The Lord is near to all who call upon Him, to all who call upon Him in truth. PSALM 145:18

He shall pray to God, and He will delight in him, He shall see His face with joy, for He restores to man His righteousness. JOB 33:26

I will call upon the Lord, who is worthy to be praised; so shall I be saved from my enemies. PSALM 18:3

"Call to Me, and I will answer you, and show you great and mighty things, which you do not know." JEREMIAH 33:3

In Praise

❧ But you are a chosen generation, a royal priesthood, a holy nation, His own special people, that you may proclaim the praises of Him who called you out of darkness into His marvelous light. 1 PETER 2:9

Oh, praise the Lord, all you Gentiles! Laud Him, all you peoples!

For His merciful kindness is great toward us, and the truth of the Lord endures forever. Praise the Lord! PSALM 117:1–2

But thanks be to God, who gives us the victory through our Lord Jesus Christ.

1 CORINTHIANS 15:57

Great is the Lord, and greatly to be praised in the city of our God, in His holy mountain.

PSALM 48:1

Oh, that men would give thanks to the Lord for His goodness, and for His wonderful works to the children of men! PSALM 107:8

Therefore by Him let us continually offer the sacrifice of praise to God, that is, the fruit of our lips, giving thanks to His name.

HEBREWS 13:15

This people I have formed for Myself; they shall declare My praise. ISAIAH 43:21

Praise the Lord! For it is good to sing praises to our God; for it is pleasant, and praise is beautiful. PSALM 147:1

I will call upon the Lord, who is worthy to be praised; so shall I be saved from my enemies. 2 SAMUEL 22:4

I will bless the Lord at all times; His praise shall continually be in my mouth. PSALM 34:1

It is good to give thanks to the Lord, and to sing praises to Your name, O Most High;
To declare Your lovingkindness in the morning, and Your faithfulness every night.

PSALM 92:1–2

To Him be the glory and the dominion forever and ever. Amen. 1 PETER 5:11

I will praise the name of God with a song, and will magnify Him with thanksgiving.

This also shall please the Lord better than an ox or bull, which has horns and hooves.

PSALM 69:30–31

Now to the King eternal, immortal, invisible, to God who alone is wise, be honor and glory forever and ever. Amen. 1 TIMOTHY 1:17

Praise the Lord, for the Lord is good; sing praises to His name, for it is pleasant.

PSALM 135:3

Because Your lovingkindness is better than life, my lips shall praise You. PSALM 63:3

And in that day you will say: "O Lord, I will praise You; though You were angry with me, Your anger is turned away, and You comfort me." ISAIAH 12:1

Let the saints be joyful in glory; let them sing aloud on their beds.

Let the high praises of God be in their mouth, and a two-edged sword in their hand.

PSALM 149:5–6

Praise the Lord! Praise God in His sanctuary; praise Him in His mighty firmament! Praise Him for His mighty acts; praise Him according to His excellent greatness!

PSALM 150:1–2

"But I will sacrifice to You with the voice of thanksgiving; I will pay what I have vowed. Salvation is of the Lord." JONAH 2:9

Sing to God, you kingdoms of the earth; oh, sing praises to the Lord, Selah. PSALM 68:32

O Lord, You are my God. I will exalt You, I will praise Your name, for You have done wonderful things; Your counsels of old are faithfulness and truth. ISAIAH 25:1

In Dedication

❧ For God is not unjust to forget your work and labor of love which you have shown toward His name, in that you have ministered to the saints, and do minister. HEBREWS 6:10

"Let your light so shine before men, that they may see your good works and glorify your Father in heaven." MATTHEW 5:16

But let each one examine his own work, and then he will have rejoicing in himself alone, and not in another. GALATIANS 6:4

My little children, let us not love in word or in tongue, but in deed and in truth. 1 JOHN 3:18

"'For I was hungry and you gave Me food; I was thirsty and you gave Me drink; I was a stranger and you took Me in;

'I was naked and you clothed Me; I was sick and you visited Me; I was in prison and you came to Me.'

"Then the righteous will answer Him, saying 'Lord, when did we see You hungry and feed You, or thirsty and give You drink?

'When did we see You a stranger and take You in, or naked and clothe You?

'Or when did we see You sick, or in prison, and come to You?'

"And the King will answer and say to them, 'Assuredly, I say to you, inasmuch as you did it to one of the least of these My brethren, you did it to Me.'" MATTHEW 25:35–40

"And whoever gives one of these little ones only a cup of cold water in the name of a disciple, assuredly, I say to you, he shall by no means lose his reward." MATTHEW 10:42

And He said to them, "Go into all the world and preach the gospel to every creature."

MARK 16:15

"You are the salt of the earth; but if the salt loses its flavor, how shall it be seasoned? It is then good for nothing but to be thrown out and trampled under foot by men.

"You are the light of the world. A city that is set on a hill cannot be hidden." MATTHEW 5:13–14

If a brother or sister is naked and destitute of daily food,

and one of you says to them, "Depart in peace, be warmed and filled," but you do not give them the things which are needed for the body, what does it profit?

Thus also faith by itself, if it does not have works, is dead. JAMES 2:15–17

By this we know love, because He laid down His life for us. And we also ought to lay down our lives for the brethren.

But whoever has this world's goods, and sees his brother in need, and shuts up his heart from him, how does the love of God abide in him? 1 JOHN 3:16–17

Pure and undefiled religion before God and the Father is this: to visit orphans and widows in their trouble, and to keep oneself unspotted from the world. JAMES 1:27

But you are a chosen generation, a royal priesthood, a holy nation, His own special people, that you may proclaim the praises of Him who called you out of darkness into His marvelous light. 1 PETER 2:9

Therefore we are ambassadors for Christ, as though God were pleading through us: we implore you on Christ's behalf, be reconciled to God. 2 CORINTHIANS 5:20

For we are His workmanship, created in Christ Jesus for good works, which God prepared beforehand that we should walk in them. EPHESIANS 2:10

Now all things are of God, who has reconciled us to Himself through Jesus Christ, and has given us the ministry of reconciliation,

2 CORINTHIANS 5:18

"You are My witnesses," says the Lord, "And My servant whom I have chosen, that you may know and believe Me, and understand that I am He. Before Me there was no God formed, nor shall there be after Me." ISAIAH 43:10

Let my heart be blameless regarding Your statutes, that I may not be ashamed.

PSALM 119:80

For the Lord is righteous, He loves righteousness; His countenance beholds the upright. PSALM 11:7

In Stewardship

But this I say: He who sows sparingly will also reap sparingly, and he who sows bountifully will also reap bountifully.

So let each one give as he purposes in his heart, not grudgingly or of necessity; for God loves a cheerful giver.

And God is able to make all grace abound toward you, that you, always having all sufficiency in all things, have an abundance for every good work. 2 CORINTHIANS 9:6–8

Honor the Lord with your possessions, and with the firstfruits of all your increase;
So your barns will be filled with plenty, and your vats will overflow with new wine.
PROVERBS 3:9–10

"Bring all the tithes into the storehouse, that there may be food in My house, and prove Me now in this," says the Lord of hosts, "if I will not open for you the windows of heaven and pour out for you such blessing that there will not be room enough to receive it.

"And I will rebuke the devourer for your sakes, so that he will not destroy the fruit of your ground, nor shall the vine fail to bear fruit for you in the field," says the Lord of hosts;

"And all nations will call you blessed, for you will be a delightful land," says the Lord of hosts. MALACHI 3:10–12

Command those who are rich in this present age not to be haughty, nor to trust in uncertain riches but in the living God, who gives us richly all things to enjoy.

Let them do good, that they be rich in good works, ready to give, willing to share,

storing up for themselves a good foundation for the time to come, that they may lay hold on eternal life. 1 TIMOTHY 6:17–19

"And whoever gives one of these little ones only a cup of cold water in the name of a disciple, assuredly, I say to you, he shall by no means lose his reward." MATTHEW 10:42

For God is not unjust to forget your work and labor of love which you have shown toward His name, in that you have ministered to the saints, and do minister. HEBREWS 6:10

There is one who scatters, yet increases more; and there is one who withholds more than is right, but it leads to poverty.

The generous soul will be made rich, and he who waters will also be watered himself.

He who diligently seeks good finds favor, but trouble will come to him who seeks evil.

PROVERBS 11:24–25,27

"Give, and it will be given to you: good measure, pressed down, shaken together, and running over will be put into your bosom. For with the same measure that you use, it will be measured back to you." LUKE 6:38

Now concerning the collection for the saints, as I have given orders to the churches of Galatia, so you must do also:

On the first day of the week let each one of you lay something aside, storing up as he may prosper, that there be no collections when I come. 1 CORINTHIANS 16:1–2

And whatever you do, do it heartily, as to the Lord and not to men,

knowing that from the Lord you will receive the reward of the inheritance; for you serve the Lord Christ. COLOSSIANS 3:23–24

"But lay up for yourselves treasures in heaven, where neither moth nor rust destroys and where thieves do not break in and steal.

"For where your treasure is, there your heart will be also." MATTHEW 6:20–21

"And everyone who has left houses or brothers or sisters or father or mother or wife or children or lands, for My name's sake, shall receive a hundredfold, and inherit everlasting life." MATTHEW 19:29

"Therefore keep the words of this covenant, and do them, that you may prosper in all that you do." DEUTERONOMY 29:9

"But seek first the kingdom of God and His righteousness, and all these things shall be added to you." MATTHEW 6:33

If they obey and serve Him, they shall spend their days in prosperity, and their years in pleasures. JOB 36:11

So Jesus answered and said, "Assuredly, I say to you, there is no one who has left house or brothers or sisters or father or mother or wife or children or lands, for My sake and the gospel's,

"who shall not receive a hundredfold now in this time—houses and brothers and sisters and mothers and children and lands, with persecutions—and in the age to come, eternal life." MARK 10:29–30

"This Book of the Law shall not depart from your mouth, but you shall meditate in it day and night, that you may observe to do according to all that is written in it. For then you will make your way prosperous, and then you will have good success." JOSHUA 1:8

In Benevolent Work

For God is not unjust to forget your work and labor of love which you have shown toward His name, in that you have ministered to the saints, and do minister. HEBREWS 6:10

"Then the King will say to those on His right hand, 'Come, you blessed of My Father, inherit the kingdom prepared for you from the foundation of the world:

'for I was hungry and you gave Me food; I was thirsty and you gave Me drink; I was a stranger and you took Me in;

'I was naked and you clothed Me; I was sick and you visited Me; I was in prison and you came to Me.'

"And the King will answer and say to them, 'Assuredly, I say to you, inasmuch as you did it to one of the least of these My brethren, you did it to Me.'" MATTHEW 25:34–36,40

But do not forget to do good and to share, for with such sacrifices God is well pleased.
HEBREWS 13:16

Command those who are rich in this present age not to be haughty, nor to trust in uncertain riches but in the living God, who gives us richly all things to enjoy.

Let them do good, that they be rich in good works, ready to give, willing to share,

storing up for themselves a good foundation for the time to come, that they may lay hold on eternal life. 1 TIMOTHY 6:17–19

"But when you do a charitable deed, do not let your left hand know what your right hand is doing,

"that your charitable deed may be in secret; and your Father who sees in secret will Himself reward you openly." MATTHEW 6:3–4

Then Jesus, looking at him, loved him, and said to him, "One thing you lack: Go your way, sell whatever you have and give to the poor, and you will have treasure in heaven; and come, take up the cross, and follow Me." MARK 10:21

"But rather give alms of such things as you have; then indeed all things are clean to you."
LUKE 11:41

He who gives to the poor will not lack, but he who hides his eyes will have many curses.
PROVERBS 28:27

I have been young, and now am old; yet I have not seen the righteous forsaken, nor his descendants begging bread.
He is ever merciful, and lends; and his descendants are blessed. PSALM 37:25–26

He who despises his neighbor sins; but he who has mercy on the poor, happy is he.
PROVERBS 14:21

And God is able to make all grace abound toward you, that you, always having all sufficiency in all things, have an abundance for every good work. 2 CORINTHIANS 9:8

He who has pity on the poor lends to the Lord, and He will pay back what he has given.

PROVERBS 19:17

My little children, let us not love in word or in tongue, but in deed and in truth.

And by this we know that we are of the truth, and shall assure our hearts before Him.

1 JOHN 3:18–19

There is one who scatters, yet increases more; and there is one who withholds more than is right, but it leads to poverty.

The generous soul will be made rich, and he who waters will also be watered himself.

He who diligently seeks good finds favor, but trouble will come to him who seeks evil.

PROVERBS 11:24–25,27

He has dispersed abroad, He has given to the poor; His righteousness endures forever; His horn will be exalted with honor. PSALM 112:9

"Give, and it will be given to you: good measure, pressed down, shaken together, and running over will be put into your bosom. For with the same measure that you use, it will be measured back to you." LUKE 6:38

Blessed is he who considers the poor; the Lord will deliver him in time of trouble.

The Lord will preserve him and keep him alive, and he will be blessed on the earth; You will not deliver him to the will of his enemies.

The Lord will strengthen him on his bed of illness; You will sustain him on his sickbed.

PSALM 41:1–3

He who has a bountiful eye will be blessed, for he gives of his bread to the poor.

PROVERBS 22:9

"You shall surely give to him, and your heart should not be grieved when you give to him, because for this thing the Lord your God will bless you in all your works and in all to which you put your hand." NUMBERS 15:10

"Sell what you have and give alms; provide yourselves money bags which do not grow old, a treasure in the heavens that does not fail, where no thief approaches nor moth destroys."

LUKE 12:33

"But when you give a feast, invite the poor, the maimed, the lame, the blind.

"And you will be blessed, because they cannot repay you; for you shall be repaid at the resurrection of the just." LUKE 14:13–14

In Obedience

❧ "He who has My commandments and keeps them, it is he who loves Me. And he who loves Me will be loved by My Father, and I will love him and manifest Myself to him." JOHN 14:21

Now by this we know that we know Him, if we keep His commandments.

He who says, "I know Him," and does not keep His commandments, is a liar, and the truth is not in him.

But whoever keeps His word, truly the love of God is perfected in him. By this we know that we are in Him.

He who says he abides in Him ought himself also to walk just as He walked.

1 JOHN 2:3–6

"Behold, I set before you today a blessing and a curse:

"the blessing, if you obey the commandments of the Lord your God which I command you today;

"and the curse, if you do not obey the commandments of the Lord your God, but turn aside from the way which I command you today, to go after other gods which you have not known." DEUTERONOMY 11:26–28

"Whoever therefore breaks one of the least of these commandments, and teaches men so, shall be called least in the kingdom of heaven; but whoever does and teaches them, he shall be called great in the kingdom of heaven."

MATTHEW 5:19

"If you keep My commandments, you will abide in My love, just as I have kept My Father's commandments and abide in His love."

JOHN 15:10

And whatever we ask we receive from Him, because we keep His commandments and do those things that are pleasing in His sight.

1 JOHN 3:22

"Therefore keep the words of this covenant, and do them, that you may prosper in all that you do." DEUTERONOMY 29:9

"For whoever does the will of My Father in heaven is My brother and sister and mother."
MATTHEW 12:50

"Oh, that they had such a heart in them that they would fear Me and always keep all My commandments, that it might be well with them and with their children forever!"
DEUTERONOMY 5:29

"If you fear the Lord and serve Him and obey His voice, and do not rebel against the commandment of the Lord, then both you and the king who reigns over you will continue following the Lord your God." 1 SAMUEL 12:14

"Not everyone who says to Me, 'Lord, Lord,' shall enter the kingdom of heaven, but he who does the will of My Father in heaven."
MATTHEW 7:21

"So you shall observe My statutes and keep My judgments, and perform them; and you will dwell in the land in safety.

"Then the land will yield its fruit, and you will eat your fill, and dwell there in safety."

LEVITICUS 25:18–19

But he who looks into the perfect law of liberty and continues in it, and is not a forgetful hearer but a doer of the work, this one will be blessed in what he does. JAMES 1:25

He who keeps the commandment keeps his soul, but he who is careless of his ways will die. PROVERBS 19:16

"Now therefore, if you will indeed obey My voice and keep My covenant, then you shall be a special treasure to Me above all people; for all the earth is Mine." EXODUS 19:5

Blessed are the undefiled in the way, who walk in the law of the Lord!
Blessed are those who keep His testimonies, who seek Him with the whole heart! PSALM 119:1–2

If you are willing and obedient, you shall eat the good of the land. ISAIAH 1:19

"And keep the charge of the Lord your God: to walk in His ways, to keep His statutes, His commandments, His judgments, and His testimonies, as it is written in the Law of Moses, that you may prosper in all that you do and wherever you turn." 1 KINGS 2:3

And the world is passing away, and the lust of it; but he who does the will of God abides forever. 1 JOHN 2:17

"If you know these things, happy are you if you do them." JOHN 13:17

In Prayer

Likewise the Spirit also helps in our weaknesses. For we do not know what we should pray for as we ought, but the Spirit Himself makes intercession for us with groanings which cannot be uttered. ROMANS 8:26

"Call to Me, and I will answer you, and show you great and mighty things, which you do not know." JEREMIAH 33:3

Then He spoke a parable to them, that men always ought to pray and not lose heart.

"And shall not God avenge His own elect who cry out day and night to Him, though He bears long with them?" LUKE 18:1,8

"Again I say to you that if two of you agree on earth concerning anything that they ask, it will be done for them by My Father in heaven.

"For where two or three are gathered together in My name, I am there in the midst of them." MATTHEW 18:19–20

"But you, when you pray, go into your room, and when you have shut your door, pray to your Father who is in the secret place; and your Father who sees in secret will reward you openly." MATTHEW 6:6

"Therefore I say to you, whatever things you ask when you pray, believe that you receive them, and you will have them." MARK 11:24

The Lord is near to all who call upon Him, to all who call upon Him in truth.

He will fulfill the desire of those who fear Him; He also will hear their cry and save them.

PSALM 145:18–19

Delight yourself also in the Lord, and He shall give you the desires of your heart.

PSALM 37:4

The Lord is far from the wicked, but He hears the prayer of the righteous. PROVERBS 15:29

Seeing then that we have a great High Priest who has passed through the heavens, Jesus the Son of God, let us hold fast our confession.

For we do not have a High Priest who cannot sympathize with our weaknesses, but was in all points tempted as we are, yet without sin.

Let us therefore come boldly to the throne of grace, that we may obtain mercy and find grace to help in time of need. HEBREWS 4:14–16

He shall pray to God, and He will delight in him, He shall see His face with joy, for He restores to man His righteousness. JOB 33:26

"For what great nation is there that has God so near to it, as the Lord our God is to us, for whatever reason we may call upon Him?"

DEUTERONOMY 4:7

For You, Lord, are good, and ready to forgive, and abundant in mercy to all those who call upon You.

In the day of my trouble I will call upon You, for You will answer me. PSALM 86:5,7

Draw near to God and He will draw near to you. Cleanse your hands, you sinners; and purify your hearts, you double-minded.

JAMES 4:8

Evening and morning and at noon I will pray, and cry aloud, and He shall hear my voice. PSALM 55:17

But without faith it is impossible to please Him, for he who comes to God must believe that He is, and that He is a rewarder of those who diligently seek Him. HEBREWS 11:6

Pray without ceasing,

in everything giving thanks; for this is the will of God in Christ Jesus for you.

1 THESSALONIANS 5:17–18

In Witness

Then Jesus came and spoke to them, saying, "All authority has been given to Me in heaven and on earth.

"Go therefore and make disciples of all the nations, baptizing them in the name of the Father and of the Son and of the Holy Spirit,

"teaching them to observe all things that I have commanded you; and lo, I am with you always, even to the end of the age." Amen.

MATTHEW 28:18–20

And He said to them, "Go into all the world and preach the gospel to every creature."

MARK 16:15

You therefore, my son, be strong in the grace that is in Christ Jesus.

And the things that you have heard from me among many witnesses, commit these to faithful men who will be able to teach others also. 2 TIMOTHY 2:1–2

Then He said to them, "Thus it is written, and thus it was necessary for the Christ to suffer and to rise from the dead the third day, "and that repentance and remission of sins should be preached in His name to all nations, beginning at Jerusalem.

"And you are witnesses of these things."

LUKE 24:46–48

And He said to them, "It is not for you to know times or seasons which the Father has put in His own authority.

"But you shall receive power when the Holy Spirit has come upon you; and you shall be witnesses to Me in Jerusalem, and in all Judea and Samaria, and to the end of the earth."

ACTS 1:7–8

Those who are wise shall shine like the brightness of the firmament, and those who turn many to righteousness like the stars forever and ever. DANIEL 12:3

Likewise you wives, be submissive to your own husbands, that even if some do not obey the word, they, without a word, may be won by the conduct of their wives. 1 PETER 3:1

But sanctify the Lord God in your hearts, and always be ready to give a defense to everyone who asks you a reason for the hope that is in you, with meekness and fear;

having a good conscience, that when they defame you as evildoers, those who revile your good conduct in Christ may be ashamed.

1 PETER 3:15–16

And you became followers of us and of the Lord, having received the word in much affliction, with joy of the Holy Spirit,

so that you became examples to all in Macedonia and Achaia who believe.

For from you the word of the Lord has sounded forth, not only in Macedonia and Achaia, but also in every place. Your faith toward God has gone out, so that we do not need to say anything. 1 THESSALONIANS 1:6–8

Ask of Me, and I will give You the nations for Your inheritance, and the ends of the earth for Your possession. PSALM 2:8

"And I, if I am lifted up from the earth, will draw all peoples to Myself." JOHN 12:32

But since we have the same spirit of faith, according to what is written, "I believed and therefore I spoke," we also believe and therefore speak. 2 CORINTHIANS 4:13

And truly Jesus did many other signs in the presence of His disciples, which are not written in this book;

but these are written that you may believe that Jesus is the Christ, the Son of God, and that believing you may have life in His name.

JOHN 20:30–31

Restore to me the joy of Your salvation, and uphold me with Your generous Spirit.

Then I will teach transgressors Your ways, and sinners shall be converted to You.

PSALM 51:12–13

The voice of one crying in the wilderness: "Prepare the way of the Lord; make straight in the desert a highway for our God.

"Every valley shall be exalted, and every mountain and hill shall be made low; the crooked places shall be made straight, and the rough places smooth;

"The glory of the Lord shall be revealed, and all flesh shall see it together; for the mouth of the Lord has spoken." ISAIAH 40:3–5

This is the disciple who testifies of these things, and wrote these things; and we know that his testimony is true.

And there are also many other things that Jesus did, which if they were written one by one, I suppose that even the world itself could not contain the books that would be written. Amen. JOHN 21:24–25

"Indeed I have given him as a witness to the people, a leader and commander for the people.

"Surely you shall call a nation you do not know, and nations who do not know you shall run to you, because of the Lord your God, and the Holy One of Israel; for He has glorified you." ISAIAH 55:4–5

Now we exhort you, brethren, warn those who are unruly, comfort the fainthearted, uphold the weak, be patient with all.

1 THESSALONIANS 5:14

Now it shall come to pass in the latter days that the mountain of the Lord's house shall be established on the top of the mountains, and shall be exalted above the hills; and all nations shall flow to it.

Many people shall come and say, "Come, and let us go up to the mountain of the Lord, to the house of the God of Jacob; He will teach us His ways, and we shall walk in His paths." For out of Zion shall go forth the law, and the word of the Lord from Jerusalem. ISAIAH 2:2–3

"And this gospel of the kingdom will be preached in all the world as a witness to all the nations, and then the end will come."

MATTHEW 24:14

From Backsliding

Behold, the Lord's hand is not shortened, that it cannot save; nor His ear heavy, that it cannot hear.

But your iniquities have separated you from your God; and your sins have hidden His face from you, so that He will not hear. ISAIAH 59:1–2

For he who lacks these things is shortsighted, even to blindness, and has forgotten that he was purged from his old sins.

Therefore, brethren, be even more diligent to make your calling and election sure, for if you do these things you will never stumble.

2 PETER 1:9–10

For whatever is born of God overcomes the world. And this is the victory that has overcome the world—our faith.

Who is he who overcomes the world, but he who believes that Jesus is the Son of God?

1 JOHN 5:4–5

Therefore submit to God. Resist the devil and he will flee from you.

Draw near to God and He will draw near to you. Cleanse your hands, you sinners; and purify your hearts, you doubleminded.

Lament and mourn and weep! Let your laughter be turned to mourning and your joy to gloom.

Humble yourselves in the sight of the Lord, and He will lift you up. JAMES 4:7–10

Then the Lord knows how to deliver the godly out of temptations and to reserve the unjust under punishment for the day of judgment. 2 PETER 2:9

Blessed is the man who endures temptation; for when he has been proved, he will receive the crown of life which the Lord has promised to those who love Him.

Let no one say when he is tempted, "I am tempted by God"; for God cannot be tempted by evil, nor does He Himself tempt anyone.

But each one is tempted when he is drawn away by his own desires and enticed.

JAMES 1:12–14

I say then: Walk in the Spirit, and you shall not fulfill the lust of the flesh. GALATIANS 5:16

If we confess our sins, He is faithful and just to forgive our sins and to cleanse us from all unrighteousness. 1 JOHN 1:9

Do not boast about tomorrow, for you do not know what a day may bring forth.

PROVERBS 27:1

Adulterers and adulteresses! Do you not know that friendship with the world is enmity with God? Whoever therefore wants to be a friend of the world makes himself an enemy of God.

Or do you think that the Scripture says in vain, "The Spirit who dwells in us yearns jealously"?

But He gives more grace. Therefore He says: "God resists the proud, but gives grace to the humble." JAMES 4:4–6

Seeing then that we have a great High Priest who has passed through the heavens, Jesus the Son of God, let us hold fast our confession.

For we do not have a High Priest who cannot sympathize with our weaknesses, but was in all points tempted as we are, yet without sin.

Let us therefore come boldly to the throne of grace, that we may obtain mercy and find grace to help in time of need. HEBREWS 4:14–16

O wretched man that I am! Who will deliver me from this body of death?

I thank God—through Jesus Christ our Lord! So then, with the mind I myself serve the law of God, but with the flesh the law of sin.

ROMANS 7:24–25

He who covers his sins will not prosper, but whoever confesses and forsakes them will have mercy. PROVERBS 28:13

No temptation has overtaken you except such as is common to man; but God is faithful, who will not allow you to be tempted beyond what you are able, but with the temptation will also make the way of escape, that you may be able to bear it. 1 CORINTHIANS 10:13

Being confident of this very thing, that He who has begun a good work in you will complete it until the day of Jesus Christ.

PHILIPPIANS 1:6

Therefore do not cast away your confidence, which has great reward.

For you have need of endurance, so that after you have done the will of God, you may receive the promise. HEBREWS 10:35–36

Therefore, brethren, be even more diligent to make your calling and election sure, for if you do these things you will never stumble.

2 PETER 1:10

The backslider in heart will be filled with his own ways, but a good man will be satisfied from above. PROVERBS 14:14

For I fear lest, when I come, I shall not find you such as I wish, and that I shall be found by such as you do not wish; lest there be contentions, jealousies, outbursts of wrath, selfish ambitions, backbitings, whisperings, conceits, tumults;

and lest, when I come again, my God will humble me among you, and I shall mourn for many who have sinned before and have not repented of the uncleanness, fornication, and licentiousness which they have practiced.

2 CORINTHIANS 12:20–21

I will heal their backsliding, I will love them freely, for My anger has turned away from him.

HOSEA 14:4

For Times of Loneliness

❧ "I will not leave you orphans; I will come to you." JOHN 14:18

God is our refuge and strength, a very present help in trouble. PSALM 46:1

"Let not your heart be troubled; you believe in God, believe also in Me." JOHN 14:1

For I am persuaded that neither death nor life, nor angels nor principalities nor powers, nor things present nor things to come,

nor height nor depth, nor any other created thing, shall be able to separate us from the love of God which is in Christ Jesus our Lord.

ROMANS 8:38–39

Casting all your care upon Him, for He cares for you. 1 PETER 5:7

The Lord also will be a refuge for the oppressed, a refuge in times of trouble.

And those who know Your name will put their trust in You; for You, Lord, have not forsaken those who seek You. PSALM 9:9–10

Let your conduct be without covetousness, and be content with such things as you have. For He Himself has said, "I will never leave you nor forsake you." HEBREWS 13:5

"Fear not, for I am with you; be not dismayed, for I am your God. I will strengthen you, yes, I will help you, I will uphold you with My righteous right hand." ISAIAH 41:10

Who shall separate us from the love of Christ? Shall tribulation, or distress, or persecution, or famine, or nakedness, or peril, or sword?

As it is written: "For Your sake we are killed all day long; we are accounted as sheep for the slaughter."

Yet in all these things we are more than conquerors through Him who loved us.

ROMANS 8:35–37

"Be strong and of good courage, do not fear nor be afraid of them; for the Lord your God,

He is the One who goes with you. He will not leave you nor forsake you." DEUTERONOMY 31:6

"Teaching them to observe all things that I have commanded you; and lo, I am with you always, even to the end of the age." Amen.
MATTHEW 28:20

I will be glad and rejoice in Your mercy, for You have considered my trouble; You have known my soul in adversities. PSALM 31:7

In all their affliction He was afflicted, and the Angel of His Presence saved them; in His love and in His pity He redeemed them; and He bore them and carried them all the days of old.
ISAIAH 63:9

For the people shall dwell in Zion at Jerusalem; you shall weep no more. He will be very gracious to you at the sound of your cry; when He hears it, He will answer you.
ISAIAH 30:19

The Lord is good, a stronghold in the day of trouble; and He knows those who trust in Him. NAHUM 1:7

Unto the upright there arises light in the darkness; He is gracious, and full of compassion, and righteous. PSALM 112:4

"Therefore you now have sorrow; but I will see you again and your heart will rejoice, and your joy no one will take from you." JOHN 16:22

As a father pities his children, so the Lord pities those who fear Him. PSALM 103:13

Cast your burden on the Lord, and He shall sustain you; He shall never permit the righteous to be moved. PSALM 55:22

For Times of Fear

"Peace I leave with you, My peace I give to you; not as the world gives do I give to you. Let not your heart be troubled, neither let it be afraid." JOHN 14:27

No evil shall befall you, nor shall any plague come near your dwelling;

For He shall give His angels charge over you, to keep you in all your ways. PSALM 91:10–11

For God has not given us a spirit of fear, but of power and of love and of a sound mind.

2 TIMOTHY 1:7

There is no fear in love; but perfect love casts out fear, because fear involves torment. But he who fears has not been made perfect in love. 1 JOHN 4:18

Yea, though I walk through the valley of the shadow of death, I will fear no evil; for You are with me; Your rod and Your staff, they comfort me.

You prepare a table before me in the presence of my enemies; You anoint my head with oil; my cup runs over. PSALM 23:4–5

For you did not receive the spirit of bondage again to fear, but you received the Spirit of adoption by whom we cry out, "Abba, Father." ROMANS 8:15

So we may boldly say: "The Lord is my helper; I will not fear. What can man do to me?"

HEBREWS 13:6

He who dwells in the secret place of the Most High shall abide under the shadow of the Almighty.

He shall cover you with His feathers, and under His wings you shall take refuge; His truth shall be your shield and buckler.

You shall not be afraid of the terror by night, nor of the arrow that flies by day,

Nor of the pestilence that walks in darkness, nor of the destruction that lays waste at noonday.

A thousand may fall at your side, and ten thousand at your right hand; but it shall not come near you. PSALM 91:1,4–7

In righteousness you shall be established; you shall be far from oppression, for you shall not fear; and from terror, for it shall not come near you. ISAIAH 54:14

When you pass through the waters, I will be with you; and through the rivers, they shall not overflow you. When you walk through the fire, you shall not be burned, nor shall the flame scorch you. ISAIAH 43:2

God is our refuge and strength, a very present help in trouble. PSALM 46:1

Behold, the Lord's hand is not shortened, that it cannot save; nor His ear heavy, that it cannot hear. ISAIAH 59:1

No evil shall befall you, nor shall any plague come near your dwelling. PSALM 91:10

The fear of man brings a snare, but whoever trusts in the Lord shall be safe.
PROVERBS 29:25

Oh, how great is Your goodness, which You have laid up for those who fear You, which You have prepared for those who trust in You in the presence of the sons of men!

You shall hide them in the secret place of Your presence from the plots of man; You shall keep them secretly in a pavilion from the strife of tongues. PSALM 31:19–20

You are my hiding place; You shall preserve me from trouble; You shall surround me with songs of deliverance. Selah. PSALM 32:7

The Lord is my light and my salvation; whom shall I fear? The Lord is the strength of my life; of whom shall I be afraid? PSALM 27:1

"No weapon formed against you shall prosper, and every tongue which rises against you in judgment you shall condemn. This is the heritage of the servants of the Lord, and their righteousness is from Me," says the Lord.

ISAIAH 54:17

"I, even I, am He who comforts you. Who are you that you should be afraid of a man who will die, and of the son of a man who will be made like grass?

"And you forget the Lord your Maker, who stretched out the heavens and laid the foundations of the earth; you have feared continually every day because of the fury of the oppressor, when he has prepared to destroy. And where is the fury of the oppressor?"

ISAIAH 51:12–13

Do not be afraid of sudden terror, nor of trouble from the wicked when it comes;

For the Lord will be your confidence, and will keep your foot from being caught.

PROVERBS 3:25–26

For Times of Anger

"Be angry, and do not sin": do not let the sun go down on your wrath. EPHESIANS 4:26

He who is slow to wrath has great understanding, but he who is impulsive exalts folly. PROVERBS 14:29

But now you must also put off all these: anger, wrath, malice, blasphemy, filthy language out of your mouth. COLOSSIANS 3:8

"But I say to you that whoever is angry with his brother without a cause shall be in danger of the judgment. And whoever says to his brother, 'Raca!' shall be in danger of the council. But whoever says, 'You fool!' shall be in danger of hell fire.

"Therefore if you bring your gift to the altar, and there remember that your brother has something against you,

"leave your gift there before the altar, and go your way. First be reconciled to your brother, and then come and offer your gift."

MATTHEW 5:22–24

Beloved, do not avenge yourselves, but rather give place to wrath; for it is written, "Vengeance is Mine, I will repay," says the Lord.

"Therefore if your enemy hungers, feed him; if he thirsts, give him a drink; for in so doing you will heap coals of fire on his head."

Do not be overcome by evil, but overcome evil with good. ROMANS 12:19–21

Let all bitterness, wrath, anger, clamor, and evil speaking be put away from you, with all malice.

And be kind to one another, tenderhearted, forgiving one another, just as God in Christ also forgave you. EPHESIANS 4:31–32

For as the churning of milk produces butter, and as wringing the nose produces blood, so the forcing of wrath produces strife.

PROVERBS 30:33

Therefore, my beloved brethren, let every man be swift to hear, slow to speak, slow to wrath;

for the wrath of man does not produce the righteousness of God. JAMES 1:19–20

A soft answer turns away wrath, but a harsh word stirs up anger.

A wrathful man stirs up strife, but he who is slow to anger allays contention.

PROVERBS 15:1,18

"For if you forgive men their trespasses, your heavenly Father will also forgive you."

MATTHEW 6:14

He who is slow to anger is better than the mighty, and he who rules his spirit than he who takes a city. PROVERBS 16:32

For we know Him who said, "Vengeance is Mine; I will repay, says the Lord." And again, "The Lord will judge His people." HEBREWS 10:30

A fool's wrath is known at once, but a prudent man covers shame. PROVERBS 12:16

Cease from anger, and forsake wrath; Do not fret—it only causes harm. PSALM 37:8

A wise man fears and departs from evil, but a fool rages and is self-confident.

He who is quick-tempered acts foolishly, and a man of wicked intentions is hated.

PROVERBS 14:16–17

An angry man stirs up strife, and a furious man abounds in transgression. PROVERBS 29:22

Do not hasten in your spirit to be angry, for anger rests in the bosom of fools.

ECCLESIASTES 7:9

Fathers, do not provoke your children, lest they become discouraged. COLOSSIANS 3:21

The discretion of a man makes him slow to anger, and it is to his glory to overlook a transgression. PROVERBS 19:11

A haughty look, a proud heart, and the plowing of the wicked are sin. PROVERBS 21:4

Scoffers ensnare a city, but wise men turn away wrath. PROVERBS 29:8

For Times of Frustration

❧ You will keep him in perfect peace, whose mind is stayed on You, because he trusts in You.
ISAIAH 26:3

Being confident of this very thing, that He who has begun a good work in you will complete it until the day of Jesus Christ.
PHILIPPIANS 1:6

Commit your way to the Lord, trust also in Him, and He shall bring it to pass. PSALM 37:5

For God has not given us a spirit of fear, but of power and of love and of a sound mind.
2 TIMOTHY 1:7

"For the Lord God will help Me; therefore I will not be disgraced; therefore I have set My face like a flint, and I know that I will not be ashamed." ISAIAH 50:7

Beloved, do not think it strange concerning the fiery trial which is to try you, as though some strange thing happened to you;

but rejoice to the extent that you partake of

Christ's sufferings, that when His glory is revealed, you may also be glad with exceeding joy. 1 PETER 4:12–13

For God is not the author of confusion but of peace, as in all the churches of the saints.
1 CORINTHIANS 14:33

For where envy and self-seeking exist, confusion and every evil thing will be there.

But the wisdom that is from above is first pure, then peaceable, gentle, willing to yield, full of mercy and good fruits, without partiality and without hypocrisy.

Now the fruit of righteousness is sown in peace by those who make peace. JAMES 3:16–18

Trust in the Lord with all your heart, and lean not on your own understanding;

In all your ways acknowledge Him, and He shall direct your paths. PROVERBS 3:5–6

If any of you lacks wisdom, let him ask of God, who gives to all liberally and without reproach, and it will be given to him. JAMES 1:5

I will instruct you and teach you in the way you should go; I will guide you with My eye.

PSALM 32:8

Great peace have those who love Your law, and nothing causes them to stumble.

PSALM 119:165

When you pass through the waters, I will be with you; and through the rivers, they shall not overflow you. When you walk through the fire, you shall not be burned, nor shall the flame scorch you. ISAIAH 43:2

Cast your burden on the Lord, and He shall sustain you; He shall never permit the righteous to be moved. PSALM 55:22

He gives power to the weak, and to those who have no might He increases strength.

Even the youths shall faint and be weary, and the young men shall utterly fall,

But those who wait on the Lord shall renew their strength; they shall mount up with wings like eagles, they shall run and not be weary, they shall walk and not faint. ISAIAH 40:29–31

Be anxious for nothing, but in everything by prayer and supplication, with thanksgiving, let your requests be made known to God;

and the peace of God, which surpasses all understanding, will guard your hearts and minds through Christ Jesus. PHILIPPIANS 4:6–7

Rest in the Lord, and wait patiently for Him; do not fret because of him who prospers in his way, because of the man who brings wicked schemes to pass. PSALM 37:7

Your ears shall hear a word behind you, saying, "This is the way, walk in it," whenever you turn to the right hand or whenever you turn to the left. ISAIAH 30:21

The steps of a good man are ordered by the Lord, and He delights in his way.

PSALM 37:23

Now this is the confidence that we have in Him, that if we ask anything according to His will, He hears us.

And if we know that He hears us, whatever we ask, we know that we have the petitions that we have asked of Him. 1 JOHN 5:14–15

The Lord will perfect that which concerns me; Your mercy, O Lord, endures forever; do not forsake the works of Your hands.

PSALM 138:8

He who did not spare His own Son, but delivered Him up for us all, how shall He not with Him also freely give us all things?

ROMANS 8:32

For Times of Guilt

❧ "Most assuredly, I say to you, he who hears My word and believes in Him who sent Me has everlasting life, and shall not come into judgment, but has passed from death into life."

JOHN 5:24

For if our heart condemns us, God is greater than our heart, and knows all things.

1 JOHN 3:20

There is therefore now no condemnation to those who are in Christ Jesus, who do not walk according to the flesh, but according to the Spirit. ROMANS 8:1

If we confess our sins, He is faithful and just to forgive us our sins and to cleanse us from all unrighteousness. 1 JOHN 1:9

"For God did not send His Son into the world to condemn the world, but that the world through Him might be saved.

"He who believes in Him is not condemned; but he who does not believe is condemned already, because he has not believed in the name of the only begotten Son of God."

JOHN 3:17–18

He will not always strive with us, nor will He keep His anger forever.

He has not dealt with us according to our sins, nor punished us according to our iniquities.

For as the heavens are high above the earth, so great is His mercy toward those who fear Him;

As far as the east is from the west, so far has He removed our transgressions from us.

PSALM 103:9–12

"For I will be merciful to their unrighteousness, and their sins and their

lawless deeds I will remember no more."
HEBREWS 8:12

"I will cleanse them from all their iniquity by which they have sinned against Me, and I will pardon all their iniquities by which they have sinned and by which they have transgressed against Me." JEREMIAH 33:8

"For if you return to the Lord, your brethren and your children will be treated with compassion by those who lead them captive, so that they may come back to this land; for the Lord your God is gracious and merciful, and will not turn His face from you if you return to Him." 2 CHRONICLES 30:9

"No more shall every man teach his neighbor, and every man his brother, saying, 'Know the Lord,' for they all shall know Me, from the least of them to the greatest of them," says the Lord. "For I will forgive their iniquity, and their sin I will remember no more."
JEREMIAH 31:34

Let us draw near with a true heart in full assurance of faith, having our hearts sprinkled from an evil conscience and our bodies washed with pure water. HEBREWS 10:22

Let the wicked forsake his way, and the unrighteous man his thoughts; let him return to the Lord, and He will have mercy on him; and to our God, for He will abundantly pardon.

ISAIAH 55:7

Therefore, if anyone is in Christ, he is a new creation; old things have passed away; behold, all things have become new.

2 CORINTHIANS 5:17

Blessed is he whose transgression is forgiven, whose sin is covered.

I acknowledged my sin to You, and my iniquity I have not hidden. I said, "I will confess my transgressions to the Lord," and You forgave the iniquity of my sin. Selah. PSALM 32:1,5

"I, even I, am He who blots out your transgressions for My own sake; and I will not remember your sins." ISAIAH 43:25

Then I heard a loud voice saying in heaven, "Now salvation, and strength, and the kingdom of our God, and the power of His Christ have come, for the accuser of our brethren, who accused them before our God day and night, has been cast down.

"And they overcame him by the blood of the Lamb and by the word of their testimony, and they did not love their lives to the death."

REVELATION 12:10–11

"Therefore I say to you, her sins, which are many, are forgiven, for she loved much. But to whom little is forgiven, the same loves little."

And He said to her, "Your sins are forgiven."

Then He said to the woman, "Your faith has saved you. Go in peace." LUKE 7:47–48,50

Who is a God like You, pardoning iniquity and passing over the transgression of the remnant of His heritage? He does not retain His anger forever, because He delights in mercy.

He will again have compassion on us, and will subdue our iniquities. You will cast all our sins into the depths of the sea. MICAH 7:18–19

Then He adds, "Their sins and their lawless deeds I will remember no more."

HEBREWS 10:17

"I have blotted out, like a thick cloud, your transgressions, and like a cloud, your sins. Return to Me, for I have redeemed you."

ISAIAH 44:22

For Times of Rebellion

❧ Likewise you younger people, submit yourselves to your elders. Yes, all of you be submissive to one another, and be clothed with humility, for "God resists the proud, but gives grace to the humble."

Therefore humble yourselves under the mighty hand of God, that He may exalt you in due time. 1 PETER 5:5–6

Therefore submit to God. Resist the devil and he will flee from you. JAMES 4:7

Let this mind be in you which was also in Christ Jesus,

who, being in the form of God, did not

consider it robbery to be equal with God,

but made Himself of no reputation, taking the form of a servant, and coming in the likeness of men.

And being found in appearance as a man, He humbled Himself and became obedient to the point of death, even the death of the cross.

PHILIPPIANS 2:5–8

Therefore gird up the loins of your mind, be sober, and rest your hope fully upon the grace that is to be brought to you at the revelation of Jesus Christ;

as obedient children, not conforming yourselves to the former lusts, as in your ignorance. 1 PETER 1:13–14

"If you are willing and obedient, you shall eat the good of the land;

"But if you refuse and rebel, you shall be devoured by the sword"; for the mouth of the Lord has spoken. ISAIAH 1:19–20

Obey those who rule over you, and be submissive, for they watch out for your souls, as those who must give account. Let them do so with joy and not with grief, for that would be unprofitable for you. HEBREWS 13:17

Then Samuel said: "Has the Lord as great delight in burnt offerings and sacrifices, as in obeying the voice of the Lord? Behold, to obey is better than sacrifice, and to heed than the fat of rams.

"For rebellion is as the sin of witchcraft, and stubbornness is as iniquity and idolatry. Because you have rejected the word of the Lord, He also has rejected you from being king." 1 SAMUEL 15:22–23

Therefore submit yourselves to every ordinance of man for the Lord's sake, whether to the king as supreme,

or to governors, as to those who are sent by him for the punishment of evildoers and for the praise of those who do good.

For this is the will of God, that by doing good you may put to silence the ignorance of foolish men. 1 PETER 2:13–15

Therefore do not let sin reign in your mortal body, that you should obey it in its lusts.

And do not present your members as instruments of unrighteousness to sin, but present yourselves to God as being alive from the dead, and your members as instruments of righteousness to God. ROMANS 6:12–13

This I say, therefore, and testify in the Lord, that you should no longer walk as the rest of the Gentiles walk, in the futility of their mind,

having their understanding darkened, being alienated from the life of God, because of the ignorance that is in them, because of the hardening of their heart. EPHESIANS 4:17–18

No grave trouble will overtake the righteous, but the wicked shall be filled with evil.

PROVERBS 12:21

For you were once darkness, but now you are light in the Lord. Walk as children of light.

Submitting to one another in the fear of God. EPHESIANS 5:8,21

Wives, submit to your own husbands, as to the Lord.

For the husband is head of the wife, as also Christ is head of the church; and He is the Savior of the body.

Therefore, just as the church is subject to Christ, so let the wives be to their own husbands in everything.

Husbands, love your wives, just as Christ also loved the church and gave Himself for it.

EPHESIANS 5:22–25

For the weapons of our warfare are not carnal but mighty in God for pulling down strongholds,

casting down arguments and every high thing that exalts itself against the knowledge of God, bringing every thought into captivity to the obedience of Christ. 2 CORINTHIANS 10:4–5

Not forsaking the assembling of ourselves together, as is the manner of some, but exhorting one another, and so much the more as you see the Day approaching. HEBREWS 10:25

Blessed are those who do His commandments, that they may have the right to the tree of life, and may enter through the gates into the city. REVELATION 22:14

"Go and proclaim these words toward the north, and say: 'Return, backsliding Israel,' says the Lord, 'and I will not cause My anger to fall on you; for I am merciful,' says the Lord, 'and I will not remain angry forever.'

"Return, you backsliding children, and I will heal your backslidings."

"Indeed we do come to You, for You are the Lord our God." JEREMIAH 3:12,22

For Times of Suffering

❧ For as the sufferings of Christ abound in us, so our consolation also abounds through Christ.

And our hope for you is steadfast, because we know that as you are partakers of the sufferings, so also you will partake of the consolation. 2 CORINTHIANS 1:5,7

"These things I have spoken to you, that in Me you may have peace. In the world you will have tribulation; but be of good cheer, I have overcome the world." JOHN 16:33

Beloved, do not think it strange concerning the fiery trial which is to try you, as though some strange thing happened to you;

but rejoice to the extent that you partake of Christ's sufferings, that when His glory is revealed, you may also be glad with exceeding joy.

If you are reproached for the name of Christ, blessed are you, for the Spirit of glory and of God rests upon you. On their part He is blasphemed, but on your part He is glorified.

1 PETER 4:12–14

For this is commendable, if because of conscience toward God one endures grief, suffering wrongfully.

For what credit is it if, when you are beaten for your faults, you take it patiently? But when you do good and suffer for it, if you take it patiently, this is commendable before God.

For to this you were called, because Christ also suffered for us, leaving us an example, that you should follow His steps. 1 PETER 2:19–21

We are confident, yes, well pleased rather to be absent from the body and to be present with the Lord.

Therefore we make it our aim, whether present or absent, to be well pleasing to Him.

For we must all appear before the judgment seat of Christ, that each one may receive the things done in the body, according to what he has done, whether good or bad.

2 CORINTHIANS 5:8–10

Is anyone among you suffering? Let him pray. Is anyone cheerful? Let him sing psalms.

JAMES 5:13

The Spirit Himself bears witness with our spirit that we are children of God, and if children, then heirs—heirs of God and joint heirs with Christ, if indeed we suffer with Him, that we may also be glorified together.

For I consider that the sufferings of this present time are not worthy to be compared with the glory which shall be revealed in us.

ROMANS 8:16–18

For He has not despised nor abhorred the affliction of the afflicted; nor has He hidden His face from Him; but when He cried to Him, He heard. PSALM 22:24

Wait on the Lord; be of good courage, and He shall strengthen your heart; wait, I say, on the Lord! PSALM 27:14

Cast your burden on the Lord, and He shall sustain you; He shall never permit the righteous to be moved. PSALM 55:22

For a righteous man may fall seven times and rise again, but the wicked shall fall by calamity. PROVERBS 24:16

And the Lord said: "I have surely seen the oppression of My people who are in Egypt, and have heard their cry because of their taskmasters, for I know their sorrows."

EXODUS 3:7

My flesh and my heart fail; but God is the strength of my heart and my portion forever.

PSALM 73:26

The Lord upholds all who fall, and raises up all those who are bowed down. PSALM 145:14

For the Lord will not cast off forever.

Though He causes grief, yet He will show compassion according to the multitude of His mercies.

For He does not afflict willingly, nor grieve the children of men. LAMENTATIONS 3:31–33

O Lord, my strength and my fortress, my refuge in the day of affliction, the Gentiles shall come to You from the ends of the earth and say, "Surely our fathers have inherited lies, worthlessness and unprofitable things."

JEREMIAH 16:19

No grave trouble will overtake the righteous, but the wicked shall be filled with evil.

PROVERBS 12:21

For His anger is but for a moment, His favor is for life; weeping may endure for a night, but joy comes in the morning. PSALM 30:5

Many are the afflictions of the righteous, but the Lord delivers him out of them all. PSALM 34:19

Why are you cast down, O my soul? And why are you disquieted within me? Hope in God; for I shall yet praise Him, the help of my countenance and my God. PSALM 42:11

You, who have shown me great and severe troubles, shall revive me again, and bring me up again from the depths of the earth. PSALM 71:20

For You will save the humble people, but will bring down haughty looks.

For You will light my lamp; the Lord my God will enlighten my darkness. PSALM 18:27–28

Those who sow in tears shall reap in joy.

He who continually goes forth weeping, bearing seed for sowing, shall doubtless come again with rejoicing, bringing his sheaves with him. PSALM 126:5–6

For Times of Discouragement

❧ Therefore do not cast away your confidence, which has great reward.

For you have need of endurance, so that after you have done the will of God, you may receive the promise. HEBREWS 10:35–36

Being confident of this very thing, that He who has begun a good work in you will complete it until the day of Jesus Christ.

PHILIPPIANS 1:6

And let us not grow weary while doing good, for in due season we shall reap if we do not lose heart. GALATIANS 6:9

I would have lost heart, unless I had believed that I would see the goodness of the Lord in the land of the living.

Wait on the Lord; be of good courage, and He shall strengthen your heart; wait, I say, on the Lord! PSALM 27:13–14

So the ransomed of the Lord shall return, and come to Zion with singing, with everlasting joy on their heads; they shall obtain joy and gladness, and sorrow and sighing shall flee away. ISAIAH 51:11

Be anxious for nothing, but in everything by prayer and supplication, with thanksgiving, let your requests be made known to God;

and the peace of God, which surpasses all understanding, will guard your hearts and minds through Christ Jesus. PHILIPPIANS 4:6–7

In this you greatly rejoice, though now for a little while, if need be, you have been grieved by various trials,

that the genuineness of your faith, being much more precious than gold that perishes, though it is tested by fire, may be found to praise, honor, and glory at the revelation of Jesus Christ,

whom having not seen you love. Though now you do not see Him, yet believing, you rejoice with joy inexpressible and full of glory,

receiving the end of your faith—the salvation of your souls. 1 PETER 1:6–9

We are hard pressed on every side, yet not crushed; we are perplexed, but not in despair;

persecuted, but not forsaken; struck down, but not destroyed. 2 CORINTHIANS 4:8–9

Though I walk in the midst of trouble, You will revive me; You will stretch out Your hand against the wrath of my enemies, and Your right hand will save me. PSALM 138:7

"Let not your heart be troubled; you believe in God, believe also in Me.

"Peace I leave with you, My peace I give to you; not as the world gives do I give to you. Let not your heart be troubled, neither let it be afraid." JOHN 14:1,27

Be of good courage, and He shall strengthen your heart, all you who hope in the Lord. PSALM 31:24

As a father pities his children, so the Lord pities those who fear Him.

For He knows our frame; He remembers that we are dust. PSALM 103:13–14

The eternal God is your refuge, and underneath are the everlasting arms; He will thrust out the enemy from before you, and will say, "Destroy!" DEUTERONOMY 33:27

Behold, God will not cast away the blameless, nor will He uphold the evildoers. JOB 8:20

But know that the Lord has set apart for Himself him who is godly; the Lord will hear when I call to Him. PSALM 4:3

For You, O Lord, will bless the righteous; with favor You will surround him as with a shield. PSALM 5:12

But now, thus says the Lord, who created you, O Jacob, and He who formed you, O Israel: "Fear not, for I have redeemed you; I have called you by your name; you are Mine." ISAIAH 43:1

So he answered, "Do not fear, for those who are with us are more than those who are with them." 2 KINGS 6:16

For the Lord loves justice, and does not forsake His saints; they are preserved forever, but the descendants of the wicked shall be cut off.

Wait on the Lord, and keep His way, and He shall exalt you to inherit the land; when the wicked are cut off, you shall see it. PSALM 37:28,34

Let us know, let us pursue the knowledge of the Lord. His going forth is established as the morning; He will come to us like the rain, like the latter and former rain to the earth.

HOSEA 6:3

So Jesus answered and said, "Assuredly, I say to you, there is no one who has left house or brothers or sisters or father or mother or wife or children or lands, for My sake and the gospel's,

"who shall not receive a hundredfold now in this time—houses and brothers and sisters and mothers and children and lands, with persecutions—and in the age to come, eternal life." MARK 10:29–30

For Times of Depression

❧ Likewise the Spirit also helps in our weaknesses. For we do not know what we should pray for as we ought, but the Spirit Himself makes intercession for us with groanings which cannot be uttered.

Now He who searches the hearts knows what the mind of the Spirit is, because He makes intercession for the saints according to the will of God. ROMANS 8:26–27

"To console those who mourn in Zion, to give them beauty for ashes, the oil of joy for mourning, the garment of praise for the spirit of heaviness; that they may be called trees of righteousness, the planting of the Lord, that He may be glorified." ISAIAH 61:3

Finally, brethren, whatever things are true, whatever things are noble, whatever things are just, whatever things are pure, whatever things are lovely, whatever things are of good report, if there is any virtue and if there is anything praiseworthy—meditate on these things.

PHILIPPIANS 4:8

Therefore humble yourselves under the mighty hand of God, that He may exalt you in due time,

casting all your care upon Him, for He cares for you. 1 PETER 5:6–7

Then He spoke a parable to them, that men always ought to pray and not lose heart.

LUKE 18:1

Beloved, do not think it strange concerning the fiery trial which is to try you, as though some strange thing happened to you;

but rejoice to the extent that you partake of Christ's sufferings, that when His glory is revealed, you may also be glad with exceeding joy. 1 PETER 4:12–13

For His anger is but for a moment, His favor is for life; weeping may endure for a night, but joy comes in the morning. PSALM 30:5

"Fear not, for I am with you; be not dismayed, for I am your God. I will strengthen you, yes, I will help you, I will uphold you with My righteous right hand." ISAIAH 41:10

So the ransomed of the Lord shall return, and come to Zion with singing, with everlasting joy on their heads; they shall obtain joy and gladness, and sorrow and sighing shall flee away. ISAIAH 51:11

"I will not leave you orphans; I will come to you." JOHN 14:18

When you pass through the waters, I will be with you; and through the rivers, they shall not overflow you. When you walk through the fire, you shall not be burned, nor shall the flame scorch you. ISAIAH 43:2

He heals the broken-hearted and binds up their wounds. PSALM 147:3

But I fear, lest somehow, as the serpent deceived Eve by his craftiness, so your minds may be corrupted from the simplicity that is in Christ.

For if he who comes preaches another Jesus whom we have not preached, or if you receive a different spirit which you have not received, or a different gospel which you have not accepted, you may well put up with it.

2 CORINTHIANS 11:3–4

For I am persuaded that neither death nor life, nor angels nor principalities nor powers, nor things present nor things to come,

nor height nor depth, nor any other created thing, shall be able to separate us from the love of God which is in Christ Jesus our Lord.

ROMANS 8:38–39

The eyes of the Lord are on the righteous, and His ears are open to their cry.

The righteous cry out, and the Lord hears, and delivers them out of all their troubles.

PSALM 34:15,17

"Can a woman forget her nursing child, and not have compassion on the son of her womb? Surely they may forget, yet I will not forget you.

"See, I have inscribed you on the palms of My hands; your walls are continually before Me." ISAIAH 49:15–16

"Blessed is the man who trusts in the Lord, and whose hope is the Lord.

"For he shall be like a tree planted by the waters, which spreads out its roots by the river, and will not fear when heat comes; but her leaf will be green, and will not be anxious in the year of drought, nor will cease from yielding fruit."

JEREMIAH 17:7–8

"And God will wipe away every tear from their eyes; there shall be no more death, nor sorrow, nor crying; and there shall be no more pain, for the former things have passed away."

REVELATION 21:4

For Times of Trouble

❧ "Let not your heart be troubled; you believe in God, believe also in Me."

"Peace I leave with you, My peace I give to you; not as the world gives do I give to you. Let not your heart be troubled, neither let it be afraid." JOHN 14:1,27

For this cause everyone who is godly shall pray to You in a time when You may be found; surely in a flood of great waters they shall not come near him.

You are my hiding place; You shall preserve me from trouble; You shall surround me with songs of deliverance. Selah. PSALM 32:6–7

God is our refuge and strength, a very present help in trouble.

Therefore we will not fear, though the earth be removed, and though the mountains be carried into the midst of the sea;

Though its waters roar and be troubled, though the mountains shake with its swelling. Selah. PSALM 46:1–3

We are hard pressed on every side, yet not crushed; we are perplexed, but not in despair;

persecuted, but not forsaken; struck down, but not destroyed. 2 CORINTHIANS 4:8–9

Blessed be the God and Father of our Lord Jesus Christ, the Father of mercies and God of all comfort,

who comforts us in all our tribulation, that we may be able to comfort those who are in any trouble, with the comfort with which we ourselves are comforted by God.

2 CORINTHIANS 1:3–4

The Lord also will be a refuge for the oppressed, a refuge in times of trouble.

PSALM 9:9

Though he fall, he shall not be utterly cast down; for the Lord upholds him with His hand.

But the salvation of the righteous is from the Lord; He is their strength in the time of trouble. PSALM 37:24,39

The wicked is ensnared by the transgression of his lips, but the righteous will come through trouble.

No grave trouble will overtake the righteous, but the wicked shall be filled with evil.

PROVERBS 12:13,21

Blessed is he who considers the poor; the Lord will deliver him in time of trouble.

PSALM 41:1

Though I walk in the midst of trouble, You will revive me; You will stretch out Your hand against the wrath of my enemies, and Your right hand will save me. PSALM 138:7

He shall deliver you in six troubles, yes, in seven no evil shall touch you. JOB 5:19

Then they cried out to the Lord in their trouble, and He saved them out of their distresses. PSALM 107:19

The Lord is good, a stronghold in the day of trouble; and He knows those who trust in Him. NAHUM 1:7

And we know that all things work together for good to those who love God, to those who are the called according to His purpose.

ROMANS 8:28

"Therefore I say to you, do not worry about your life, what you will eat or what you will drink; nor about your body, what you will put on. Is not life more than food and the body more than clothing?

"Look at the birds of the air, for they neither sow nor reap nor gather into barns; yet your heavenly Father feeds them. Are you not of more value than they?

"Which of you by worrying can add one cubit to his stature?

"So why do you worry about clothing? Consider the lilies of the field, how they grow: they neither toil nor spin;

"and yet I say to you that even Solomon in all his glory was not arrayed like one of these.

"Now if God so clothes the grass of the field, which today is, and tomorrow is thrown into the oven, will He not much more clothe you, O you of little faith?

"Therefore do not worry, saying, 'What shall we eat?' or 'What shall we drink?' or 'What shall we wear?'

"For after all these things the Gentiles seek. For your heavenly Father knows that you need all these things.

"But seek first the kingdom of God and His righteousness, and all these things shall be added to you.

"Therefore do not worry about tomorrow, for tomorrow will worry about its own things. Sufficient for the day is its own trouble."

MATTHEW 6:25–34

Be anxious for nothing, but in everything by prayer and supplication, with thanksgiving, let your requests be made known to God;

and the peace of God, which surpasses all understanding, will guard your hearts and minds through Christ Jesus. PHILIPPIANS 4:6–7

For Times of Need

❧ Though the fig tree may not blossom, nor fruit be on the vines; though the labor of the olive may fail, and the fields yield no food; though the flock be cut off from the fold, and there be no herd in the stalls—

Yet I will rejoice in the Lord, I will joy in the God of my salvation. HABAKKUK 3:17–18

"Therefore do not worry, saying, 'What shall we eat?' or 'What shall we drink?' or 'What shall we wear?'

"For after all these things the Gentiles seek. For your heavenly Father knows that you need all these things.

"But seek first the kingdom of God and His righteousness, and all these things shall be added to you." MATTHEW 6:31–33

The Lord is my shepherd; I shall not want.
PSALM 23:1

Behold, the eye of the Lord is on those who fear Him, on those who hope in His mercy,

To deliver their soul from death, and to keep them alive in famine. PSALM 33:18–19

"I will deliver you from all your uncleannesses. I will call for the grain and multiply it, and bring no famine upon you.

"And I will multiply the fruit of your trees and the increase of your fields, so that you need never again bear the reproach of famine among the nations." EZEKIEL 36:29–30

Ask the Lord for rain in the time of the latter rain. The Lord will make flashing clouds; He will give them showers of rain, grass in the field for everyone. ZECHARIAH 10:1

For He satisfies the longing soul, and fills the hungry soul with goodness. PSALM 107:9

But He answered and said, "It is written, 'Man shall not live by bread alone, but by every word that proceeds from the mouth of God.'"

MATTHEW 4:4

They shall not be ashamed in the evil time, and in the days of famine they shall be satisfied.

PSALM 37:19

"When the poor and needy seek water, and there is none, and their tongues fail for thirst, I, the Lord, will hear them; I, the God of Israel, will not forsake them." ISAIAH 41:17

For the needy shall not always be forgotten; the expectation of the poor shall not perish forever. PSALM 9:18

The firstborn of the poor will feed, and the needy will lie down in safety; I will kill your roots with famine, and it will slay your remnant.
ISAIAH 14:30

Your congregation dwelt in it; You, O God, provided from Your goodness for the poor.
PSALM 68:10

But He saves the needy from the sword, from the mouth of the mighty, and from their hand.

So the poor have hope, and injustice shuts her mouth. JOB 5:15–16

He raises the poor out of the dust, and lifts the needy out of the ash heap. PSALM 113:7

He shall regard the prayer of the destitute, and shall not despise their prayer. PSALM 102:17

Listen, my beloved brethren: Has God not chosen the poor of this world to be rich in faith and heirs of the kingdom which He promised to those who love Him? JAMES 2:5

"But Abraham said, 'Son, remember that in your lifetime you received your good things, and likewise Lazarus evil things; but now he is comforted and you are tormented.'" LUKE 16:25

Sing to the Lord! Praise the Lord! For He has delivered the life of the poor from the hand of evildoers. JEREMIAH 20:13

For Times of Temptation

O wretched man that I am! Who will deliver me from this body of death? I thank God—through Jesus Christ our Lord!

So then, with the mind I myself serve the law of God, but with the flesh the law of sin.

ROMANS 7:24–25

No temptation has overtaken you except such as is common to man; but God is faithful, who will not allow you to be tempted beyond what you are able, but with the temptation will also make the way of escape, that you may be able to bear it. 1 CORINTHIANS 10:13

I say then: Walk in the Spirit, and you shall not fulfill the lust of the flesh. GALATIANS 5:16

For in that He Himself has suffered, being tempted, He is able to aid those who are tempted. HEBREWS 2:18

Then the Lord knows how to deliver the godly out of temptations and to reserve the unjust under punishment for the day of judgment. 2 PETER 2:9

You are of God, little children, and have overcome them, because He who is in you is greater than he who is in the world. 1 JOHN 4:4

My brethren, count it all joy when you fall into various trials,

knowing that the testing of your faith produces patience. JAMES 1:2–3

Knowing this, that our old man was crucified with Him, that the body of sin might be done away with, that we should no longer be slaves of sin.

For sin shall not have dominion over you, for you are not under law but under grace.

ROMANS 6:6,14

In this you greatly rejoice, though now for a little while, if need be, you have been grieved by various trials,

that the genuineness of your faith, being much more precious than gold that perishes, though it is tested by fire, may be found to praise, honor, and glory at the revelation of Jesus Christ. 1 PETER 1:6–7

Yet in all these things we are more than conquerors through Him who loved us.

ROMANS 8:37

"These things I have spoken to you, that in Me you may have peace. In the world you will have tribulation; but be of good cheer, I have overcome the world." JOHN 16:33

Finally, my brethren, be strong in the Lord and in the power of His might.

Put on the whole armor of God, that you

may be able to stand against the wiles of the devil.

Above all, taking the shield of faith with which you will be able to quench all the fiery darts of the wicked one. EPHESIANS 6:10–11,16

Who gave Himself for our sins, that He might deliver us from this present evil age, according to the will of our God and Father.
GALATIANS 1:4

Therefore submit to God. Resist the devil and he will flee from you. JAMES 4:7

"And I will put enmity between you and the woman, and between your seed and her Seed; He shall bruise your head, and you shall bruise His heel." GENESIS 3:15

Blessed is the man who endures temptation; for when he has been proved, he will receive the crown of life which the Lord has promised to those who love Him.

Let no one say when he is tempted, "I am tempted by God"; for God cannot be tempted by evil, nor does He Himself tempt anyone.

But each one is tempted when he is drawn away by his own desires and enticed.

JAMES 1:12–14

And the Lord said, "Simon, Simon! Indeed, Satan has asked for you, that he may sift you as wheat.

"But I have prayed for you, that your faith should not fail; and when you have returned to Me, strengthen your brethren." LUKE 22:31–32

For whatever is born of God overcomes the world. And this is the victory that has overcome the world—our faith.

Who is he who overcomes the world, but he who believes that Jesus is the Son of God?

1 JOHN 5:4–5

Be sober, be vigilant; because your adversary the devil walks about like a roaring lion, seeking whom he may devour.

Resist him, steadfast in the faith, knowing that the same sufferings are experienced by your brotherhood in the world. 1 PETER 5:8–9

"I do not pray that You should take them out of the world, but that You should keep them from the evil one." JOHN 17:15

But God forbid that I should glory except in the cross of our Lord Jesus Christ, by whom the world has been crucified to me, and I to the world. GALATIANS 6:14

And the God of peace will crush Satan under your feet shortly. The grace of our Lord Jesus Christ be with you. Amen. ROMANS 16:20

For Times of Impatience

That you do not become sluggish, but imitate those who through faith and patience inherit the promises. HEBREWS 6:12

And not only that, but we also glory in tribulations, knowing that tribulation produces perseverance;

and perseverance, character; and character, hope.

Now hope does not disappoint, because the love of God has been poured out in our hearts by the Holy Spirit who was given to us.

ROMANS 5:3–5

For whatever things were written before were written for our learning, that we through the patience and comfort of the Scriptures might have hope.

Now may the God of patience and comfort grant you to be like-minded toward one another, according to Christ Jesus. ROMANS 15:4–5

Therefore we also, since we are surrounded by so great a cloud of witnesses, let us lay aside every weight, and the sin which so easily ensnares us, and let us run with endurance the race that is set before us.

HEBREWS 12:1

Knowing that the testing of your faith produces patience.

But let patience have its perfect work, that you may be perfect and complete, lacking nothing. JAMES 1:3–4

Therefore do not cast away your confidence, which has great reward.

For you have need of endurance, so that after you have done the will of God, you may receive the promise:

"For yet a little while, and He who is coming will come and will not tarry." HEBREWS 10:35–37

Therefore be patient, brethren, until the coming of the Lord. See how the farmer waits for the precious fruit of the earth, waiting patiently for it until it receives the early and latter rain.

You also be patient. Establish your hearts, for the coming of the Lord is at hand.

JAMES 5:7–8

I waited patiently for the Lord; and He inclined to me, and heard my cry. PSALM 40:1

Rest in the Lord, and wait patiently for Him; do not fret because of him who prospers in his way, because of the man who brings wicked schemes to pass.

Cease from anger, and forsake wrath; do not fret—it only causes harm.

For evildoers shall be cut off; but those who wait on the Lord, they shall inherit the earth.

PSALM 37:7–9

But the fruit of the Spirit is love, joy, peace, longsuffering, kindness, goodness, faithfulness.

GALATIANS 5:22

"But the ones that fell on the good ground are those who, having heard the word with a noble and good heart, keep it and bear fruit with patience." LUKE 8:15

It is good that one should hope and wait quietly for the salvation of the Lord.
LAMENTATIONS 3:26

"In your patience possess your souls."
LUKE 21:19

"Kings shall be your foster fathers, and their queens your nursing mothers; they shall bow down to you with their faces to the earth, and lick up the dust of your feet. Then you will know that I am the Lord, for they shall not be ashamed who wait for Me." ISAIAH 49:23

Eternal life to those who by patient continuance in doing good seek for glory, honor, and immortality. ROMANS 2:7

You will keep him in perfect peace, whose mind is stayed on You, because he trusts in You.
Trust in the Lord forever, for in YAH, the Lord, is everlasting strength. ISAIAH 26:3–4

But if we hope for what we do not see, then we eagerly wait for it with perseverance.

ROMANS 8:25

And it will be said in that day: "Behold, this is our God; we have waited for Him, and He will save us. This is the Lord; we have waited for Him; we will be glad and rejoice in His salvation." ISAIAH 25:9

For Times of Sickness

Is anyone among you sick? Let him call for the elders of the church, and let them pray over him, anointing him with oil in the name of the Lord.

And the prayer of faith will save the sick, and the Lord will raise him up. And if he has committed sins, he will be forgiven. JAMES 5:14–15

And said, "If you diligently heed the voice of the Lord your God and do what is right in His sight, give ear to His commandments and keep all His statutes, I will put none of the diseases on you which I have brought on the Egyptians. For I am the Lord who heals you." EXODUS 15:26

Who forgives all your iniquities, who heals all your diseases,

Who redeems your life from destruction, who crowns you with lovingkindness and tender mercies,

Who satisfies your mouth with good things, so that your youth is renewed like the eagle's.

PSALM 103:3–5

Surely He shall deliver you from the snare of the fowler and from the perilous pestilence.

You shall not be afraid of the terror by night, nor of the arrow that flies by day,

Nor of the pestilence that walks in darkness, nor of the destruction that lays waste at noonday.

No evil shall befall you, nor shall any plague come near your dwelling. PSALM 91:3,5–6,10

"So you shall serve the Lord your God, and He will bless your bread and your water. And I will take sickness away from the midst of you."

EXODUS 23:25

The Lord will strengthen him on his bed of illness; you will sustain him on his sickbed.

PSALM 41:3

"Behold, I will bring it health and healing; I will heal them and reveal to them the abundance of peace and truth." JEREMIAH 33:6

But He was wounded for our transgressions, He was bruised for our iniquities; the chastisement for our peace was upon Him, and by His stripes we are healed.
ISAIAH 53:5

Who Himself bore our sins in His own body on the tree, that we, having died to sins, might live for righteousness—by whose stripes you were healed. 1 PETER 2:24

Beloved, I pray that you may prosper in all things and be in health, just as your soul prospers. 3 JOHN 1:2

He sent His word and healed them, and delivered them from their destructions.
PSALM 107:20

And Jesus went about all the cities and villages, teaching in their synagogues, preaching the gospel of the kingdom, and healing every sickness and every disease among the people.
MATTHEW 9:35

O Lord my God, I cried out to You, and You have healed me. PSALM 30:2

Heal me, O Lord, and I shall be healed; save me, and I shall be saved, for You are my praise. JEREMIAH 17:14

And the whole multitude sought to touch Him, for power went out from Him and healed them all. LUKE 6:19

"For I will restore health to you and heal you of your wounds," says the Lord, "because they called you an outcast saying: 'This is Zion; no one seeks her.'" JEREMIAH 30:17

Come, and let us return to the Lord; for He has torn, but He will heal us; He has stricken, but He will bind us up. HOSEA 6:1

My son, give attention to my words; incline your ear to my sayings.

Do not let them depart from your eyes; keep them in the midst of your heart;

For they are life to those who find them, and health to all their flesh. PROVERBS 4:20–22

For Times of Sadness

"The Spirit of the Lord God is upon Me, because the Lord has anointed Me to preach good tidings to the poor; He has sent Me to heal the brokenhearted, to proclaim liberty to the captives, and the opening of the prison to those who are bound;

"To proclaim the acceptable year of the Lord, and the day of vengeance of our God; to comfort all who mourn,

"To console those who mourn in Zion, to give them beauty for ashes, the oil of joy for mourning, the garment of praise for the spirit of heaviness; that they may be called trees of righteousness, the planting of the Lord, that He may be glorified." ISAIAH 61:1–3

Blessed are those who mourn, for they shall be comforted. MATTHEW 5:4

Now may our Lord Jesus Christ Himself, and our God and Father, who has loved us and given us everlasting consolation and good hope by grace,

comfort your hearts and establish you in every good word and work.

2 THESSALONIANS 2:16–17

"Most assuredly, I say to you that you will weep and lament, but the world will rejoice; and you will be sorrowful, but your sorrow will be turned into joy.

"A woman, when she is in labor, has sorrow because her hour has come; but as soon as she has given birth to the child, she no longer remembers the anguish, for joy that a human being has been born into the world.

"Therefore you now have sorrow; but I will see you again and your heart will rejoice, and your joy no one will take from you." JOHN 16:20–22

You shall no longer be termed Forsaken, nor shall your land any more be termed Desolate; but you shall be called Hephzibah, and your land Beulah; for the Lord delights in you, and your land shall be married. ISAIAH 62:4

When you pass through the waters, I will be with you; and through the rivers, they shall not overflow you. When you walk through the fire, you shall not be burned, nor shall the flame scorch you. ISAIAH 43:2

This is my comfort in my affliction, for Your word has given me life. PSALM 119:50

So the ransomed of the Lord shall return, and come to Zion with singing, with everlasting joy on their heads; they shall obtain joy and gladness, and sorrow and sighing shall flee away. ISAIAH 51:11

For we do not have a High Priest who cannot sympathize with our weaknesses, but was in all points tempted as we are, yet without sin.

Let us therefore come boldly to the throne of grace, that we may obtain mercy and find grace to help in time of need. HEBREWS 4:15–16

Blessed be the God and Father of our Lord Jesus Christ, the Father of mercies and God of all comfort,

who comforts us in all our tribulation, that we may be able to comfort those who are in any trouble, with the comfort with which we ourselves are comforted by God.

2 CORINTHIANS 1:3–4

And those who know Your name will put their trust in You; for You, Lord, have not forsaken those who seek You. PSALM 9:10

When my father and my mother forsake me, then the Lord will take care of me.

PSALM 27:10

Persecuted, but not forsaken; struck down, but not destroyed. 2 CORINTHIANS 4:9

I have been young, and now am old; yet I have not seen the righteous forsaken, nor his descendants begging bread. PSALM 37:25

"When the poor and needy seek water, and there is none, and their tongues fail for thirst, I, the Lord, will hear them; I, the God of Israel, will not forsake them." ISAIAH 41:17

Because he has set his love upon Me, therefore I will deliver him; I will set him on high, because he has known My name.

He shall call upon Me, and I will answer him; I will be with him in trouble; I will deliver him and honor him. PSALM 91:14–15

But as it is written: "Eye has not seen, nor ear heard, nor have entered into the heart of man the things which God has prepared for those who love Him." 1 CORINTHIANS 2:9

For Times of Bereavement

But I do not want you to be ignorant, brethren, concerning those who have fallen asleep, lest you sorrow as others who have no hope.

For if we believe that Jesus died and rose again, even so God will bring with Him those who sleep in Jesus. 1 THESSALONIANS 4:13–14

Yea, though I walk through the valley of the shadow of death, I will fear no evil; for You are with me; Your rod and Your staff, they comfort me. PSALM 23:4

For we know that if our earthly house, this tent, is destroyed, we have a building from God, a house not made with hands, eternal in the heavens.

For in this we groan, earnestly desiring to be clothed with our habitation which is from heaven,

if indeed, having been clothed, we shall not be found naked.

For we who are in this tent groan, being burdened, not because we want to be unclothed, but further clothed, that mortality may be swallowed up by life. 2 CORINTHIANS 5:1–4

"And God will wipe away every tear from their eyes; there shall be no more death, nor sorrow, nor crying; and there shall be no more pain, for the former things have passed away."
REVELATION 21:4

Now He who has prepared us for this very thing is God, who also has given us the Spirit as a guarantee.

Therefore we are always confident, knowing that while we are at home in the body we are absent from the Lord.

For we walk by faith, not by sight.

We are confident, yes, well pleased rather to be absent from the body and to be present with the Lord. 2 CORINTHIANS 5:5–8

So the ransomed of the Lord shall return, and come to Zion with singing, with everlasting joy on their heads; they shall obtain joy and gladness, and sorrow and sighing shall flee away. ISAIAH 51:11

"O Death, where is your sting? O Hades, where is your victory?"

The sting of death is sin, and the strength of sin is the law.

But thanks be to God, who gives us the victory through our Lord Jesus Christ.

1 CORINTHIANS 15:55–57

Blessed be the God and Father of our Lord Jesus Christ, the Father of mercies and God of all comfort,

who comforts us in all our tribulation, that we may be able to comfort those who are in any trouble, with the comfort with which we ourselves are comforted by God.

2 CORINTHIANS 1:3–4

But as it is written: "Eye has not seen, nor ear heard, nor have entered into the heart of man the things which God has prepared for those who love Him." 1 CORINTHIANS 2:9

"And you will be blessed, because they cannot repay you; for you shall be repaid at the resurrection of the just." LUKE 14:14

He will redeem his soul from going down to the Pit, and his life shall see the light. JOB 33:28

Precious in the sight of the Lord is the death of His saints. PSALM 116:15

"The Lord kills and makes alive; He brings down to the grave and brings up." 1 SAMUEL 2:6

Our God is the God of salvation; and to God the Lord belong escapes from death. PSALM 68:20

For since by man came death, by Man also came the resurrection of the dead.

For as in Adam all die, even so in Christ all shall be made alive. 1 CORINTHIANS 15:21–22

Jesus said to her, "I am the resurrection and the life. He who believes in Me, though he may die, he shall live." JOHN 11:25

Blessed are those who mourn, for they shall be comforted. MATTHEW 5:4

Sing, O heavens! Be joyful, O earth! And break out in singing, O mountains! For the Lord has comforted His people, and will have mercy on His afflicted. ISAIAH 49:13

Then his servants said to him, "What is this that you have done? You fasted and wept for the child while he was alive, but when the child died, you arose and ate food."

So he said, "While the child was still alive, I fasted and wept; for I said, 'Who can tell whether the Lord will be gracious to me, that the child may live?'

"But now he is dead; why should I fast? Can I bring him back again? I shall go to him, but he shall not return to me." 2 SAMUEL 12:21–23

PROMISES FOR YOUR FAMILY

Wives

He who finds a wife finds a good thing, and obtains favor from the Lord. PROVERBS 18:22

Wives, submit to your own husbands, as to the Lord.

For the husband is head of the wife, as also Christ is head of the church; and He is the Savior of the body.

Therefore, just as the church is subject to Christ, so let the wives be to their own husbands in everything. EPHESIANS 5:22–24

Likewise you wives, be submissive to your own husbands, that even if some do not obey the word, they, without a word, may be won by the conduct of their wives,

when they observe your chaste conduct accompanied by fear.

Do not let your beauty be that outward adorning of arranging the hair, of wearing gold, or of putting on fine apparel;

but let it be the hidden person of the heart, with the incorruptible ornament of a gentle and quiet spirit, which is very precious in the sight of God.

For in this manner, in former times, the holy women who trusted in God also adorned themselves, being submissive to their own husbands,

as Sarah obeyed Abraham, calling him lord, whose daughters you are if you do good and are not afraid with any terror. 1 PETER 3:1–6

Wives, submit to your own husbands, as is fitting in the Lord. COLOSSIANS 3:18

Your wife shall be like a fruitful vine in the very heart of your house, your children like olive plants all around your table. PSALM 128:3

Let the husband render to his wife the affection due her, and likewise also the wife to her husband. 1 CORINTHIANS 7:3

Who can find a virtuous wife? For her worth is far above rubies.

The heart of her husband safely trusts her; so he will have no lack of gain.

She does him good and not evil all the days of her life.

She seeks wool and flax, and willingly works with her hands.

She is like the merchant ships, she brings her food from afar.

She also rises while it is yet night, and provides food for her household, and a portion for her maidservants.

She considers a field and buys it; from her profits she plants a vineyard.

She girds herself with strength, and strengthens her arms.

She perceives that her merchandise is good, and her lamp does not go out by night.

She stretches out her hands to the distaff, and her hand holds the spindle.

She extends her hand to the poor, yes, she reaches out her hands to the needy.

She is not afraid of snow for her household, for all her household is clothed with scarlet.

She makes tapestry for herself; her clothing is fine linen and purple.

Her husband is known in the gates, when he sits among the elders of the land.

She makes linen garments and sells them, and supplies sashes for the merchants.

Strength and honor are her clothing; she shall rejoice in time to come.

She opens her mouth with wisdom, and on her tongue is the law of kindness.

She watches over the ways of her household, and does not eat the bread of idleness.

Her children rise up and call her blessed; her husband also, and he praises her:

"Many daughters have done well, but you excel them all."

Charm is deceitful and beauty is vain, but a woman who fears the Lord, she shall be praised.

Give her of the fruit of her hands, and let her own works praise her in the gates.

PROVERBS 31:10–31

An excellent wife is the crown of her husband, but she who causes shame is like rottenness in his bones. PROVERBS 12:4

Let your fountain be blessed, and rejoice with the wife of your youth.

As a loving deer and a graceful doe, let her breasts satisfy you at all times; and always be enraptured with her love. PROVERBS 5:18–19

Every wise woman builds her house, but the foolish pulls it down with her hands.

PROVERBS 14:1

Houses and riches are an inheritance from fathers, but a prudent wife is from the Lord.

PROVERBS 19:14

Husbands

Husbands, love your wives and do not be bitter toward them.

Children, obey your parents in all things, for this is well pleasing to the Lord.

COLOSSIANS 3:19–20

Let the husband render to his wife the affection due her, and likewise also the wife to her husband. 1 CORINTHIANS 7:3

Your wife shall be like a fruitful vine in the very heart of your house, your children like olive plants all around your table.

Behold, thus shall the man be blessed who fears the Lord. PSALM 128:3–4

But if anyone does not provide for his own, and especially for those of his household, he has denied the faith and is worse than an unbeliever. 1 TIMOTHY 5:8

Live joyfully with the wife whom you love all the days of your vain life which He has given you under the sun, all your days of vanity; for that is your portion in life, and in the labor which you perform under the sun.

ECCLESIASTES 9:9

But I want you to know that the head of every man is Christ, the head of woman is man, and the head of Christ is God. 1 CORINTHIANS 11:3

Let your foundation be blessed, and rejoice with the wife of your youth.

As a loving deer and a graceful doe, let her breasts satisfy you at all times; and always be enraptured with her love. PROVERBS 5:18–19

"For I have known him, in order that he may command his children and his household after him, that they keep the way of the Lord, to do righteousness and justice, that the Lord may bring to Abraham what He has spoken to him."

GENESIS 18:19

Likewise you husbands, dwell with them with understanding, giving honor to the wife, as to the weaker vessel, and as being heirs together of the grace of life, that your prayers may not be hindered. 1 PETER 3:7

Husbands, love your wives, just as Christ also loved the church and gave Himself for it,

that He might sanctify and cleanse it with the washing of water by the word,

that He might present it to Himself a glorious church, not having spot or wrinkle or any such thing, but that it should be holy and without blemish.

So husbands ought to love their own wives as their own bodies; he who loves his wife loves himself.

For no one ever hated his own flesh, but nourishes and cherishes it, just as the Lord does the church.

For we are members of His body, of His flesh and of His bones.

"For this reason a man shall leave his father and mother and be joined to his wife, and the two shall become one flesh."

This is a great mystery, but I speak concerning Christ and the church.

Nevertheless let each one of you in particular so love his own wife as himself, and let the wife see that she respects her husband.

EPHESIANS 5:25–33

Behold, children are a heritage from the Lord, the fruit of the womb is His reward.

Like arrows in the hand of a warrior, so are the children of one's youth.

Happy is the man who has his quiver full of them; they shall not be ashamed, but shall speak with their enemies in the gate.

PSALM 127:3–5

Children's children are the crown of old men, and the glory of children is their father.

PROVERBS 17:6

A good man leaves an inheritance to his children's children, but the wealth of the sinner is stored up for the righteous.

He who spares his rod hates his son, but he who loves him disciplines him promptly.

PROVERBS 13:22,24

As a father pities his children, so the Lord pities those who fear Him. PSALM 103:13

"And these words which I command you today shall be in your heart;

"you shall teach them diligently to your children, and shall talk of them when you sit in your house, when you walk by the way, when you lie down, and when you rise up.

"You shall bind them as a sign on your hand, and they shall be as frontlets between your eyes.

"You shall write them on the doorposts of your house and on your gates."

DEUTERONOMY 6:6–9

A wise son makes a father glad, but a foolish man despises his mother. PROVERBS 15:20

The father of the righteous will greatly rejoice, and he who begets a wise child will delight in him. PROVERBS 23:24

Fathers, do not provoke your children, lest they become discouraged. COLOSSIANS 3:21

Parents

"And if it seems evil to you to serve the Lord, choose for yourselves this day whom you will serve, whether the gods which your fathers served that were on the other side of the River, or the gods of the Amorites, in whose land you dwell. But as for me and my house, we will serve the Lord." JOSHUA 24:15

Fathers, do not provoke your children, lest they become discouraged. COLOSSIANS 3:21

"And these words which I command you today shall be in your heart;

"you shall teach them diligently to your children, and shall talk of them when you sit in your house, when you walk by the way, when you lie down, and when you rise up.

"You shall bind them as a sign on your hand, and they shall be as frontlets between your eyes.

"You shall write them on the doorposts of your house and on your gates."

DEUTERONOMY 6:6–9

Train up a child in the way he should go, and when he is old he will not depart from it.

PROVERBS 22:6

"For I have known him, in order that he may command his children and his household after him, that they keep the way of the Lord, to do righteousness and justice, that the Lord may bring to Abraham what He has spoken to him."

GENESIS 18:19

"Honor your father and your mother, that your days may be long upon the land which the Lord your God is giving you." EXODUS 20:12

Blessed is every one who fears the Lord, who walks in His ways.

When you eat the labor of your hands, you shall be happy, and it shall be well with you.

Your wife shall be like a fruitful vine in the very heart of your house, your children like olive plants all around your table.

Behold, thus shall the man be blessed who fears the Lord. PSALM 128:1–4

Now for the third time I am ready to come to you. And I will not be burdensome to you; for I do not seek yours, but you. For the children ought not to lay up for the parents, but the parents for the children. 2 CORINTHIANS 12:14

And you, fathers, do not provoke your children to wrath, but bring them up in the training and admonition of the Lord.

EPHESIANS 6:4

"The Lord your God will make you abound in all the work of your hand, in the fruit of your body, in the increase of your livestock, and in the produce of your land for good. For the Lord will again rejoice over you for good as He rejoiced over your fathers." DEUTERONOMY 30:9

May the Lord give you increase more and more, you and your children. PSALM 115:14

"And he arose and came to his father. But when he was still a great way off, his father saw him and had compassion, and ran and fell on his neck and kissed him.

"And the son said to him, 'Father, I have sinned against heaven and in your sight, and am no longer worthy to be called your son.'

"But the father said to his servants, 'Bring out the best robe and put it on him, and put a ring on his hand and sandals on his feet.

'And bring the fatted calf here and kill it, and let us eat and be merry;

'for this my son was dead and is alive again; he was lost and is found.' And they began to be merry." LUKE 15:20–24

Wives, submit to your own husbands, as to the Lord.

For the husband is head of the wife, as also Christ is head of the church; and He is the Savior of the body.

Therefore, just as the church is subject to Christ, so let the wives be to their own husbands in everything.

Husbands, love your wives, just as Christ also loved the church and gave Himself for it,

that He might sanctify and cleanse it with the washing of water by the word, that He might present it to Himself a glorious church, not having spot or wrinkle or any such thing, but that it should be holy and without blemish.

So husbands ought to love their own wives as their own bodies; he who loves his wife loves himself. EPHESIANS 5:22–28

"And He will love you and bless you and multiply you; He will also bless the fruit of your womb and the fruit of your land, your grain and your new wine and your oil, the increase of your cattle and the offspring of your flock, in the land of which He swore to your fathers to give you." DEUTERONOMY 7:13

Behold, children are a heritage from the Lord, the fruit of the womb is His reward.

Like arrows in the hand of a warrior, so are the children of one's youth.

Happy is the man who has his quiver full of them; they shall not be ashamed, but shall speak with their enemies in the gate.

PSALM 127:3–5

Your wife shall be like a fruitful vine in the

very heart of your house, your children like olive plants all around your table.

Behold, thus shall the man be blessed who fears the Lord.

The Lord bless you out of Zion, and may you see the good of Jerusalem all the days of your life.

Yes, may you see your children's children. Peace be upon Israel! PSALM 128:3–6

"And he will turn the hearts of the fathers to the children, and the hearts of the children to their fathers, lest I come and strike the earth with a curse." MALACHI 4:6

Foolishness is bound up in the heart of a child, but the rod of correction will drive it far from him. PROVERBS 22:15

Do not withhold correction from a child, for if you beat him with a rod, he will not die.

You shall beat him with a rod, and deliver his soul from hell. PROVERBS 23:13–14

The rod and reproof give wisdom, but a child left to himself brings shame to his mother.

Correct your son, and he will give you rest; yes, he will give delight to your soul.

PROVERBS 29:15,17

Children

Children, obey your parents in all things, for this is well pleasing to the Lord.

COLOSSIANS 3:20

"Honor your father and your mother, as the Lord your God has commanded you, that your days may be long, and that it may be well with you in the land which the Lord your God is giving you." DEUTERONOMY 5:16

Remember now your Creator in the days of your youth, before the difficult days come, and the years draw near when you say, "I have no pleasure in them." ECCLESIASTES 12:1

Listen to your father who begot you, and do not despise your mother when she is old.

The father of the righteous will greatly rejoice, and he who begets a wise child will delight in him.

Let your father and your mother be glad, and let her who bore you rejoice.

PROVERBS 23:22,24–25

Children, obey your parents in the Lord, for this is right.

"Honor your father and mother," which is the first commandment with promise:

"that it may be well with you and you may live long on the earth." EPHESIANS 6:1–3

My son, do not forget my law, but let your heart keep my commands;

For length of days and long life and peace they will add to you.

Let not mercy and truth forsake you; bind them around your neck, write them on the tablet of your heart,

And so find favor and high esteem in the sight of God and man. PROVERBS 3:1–4

It is good for a man to bear the yoke in his youth. LAMENTATIONS 3:27

My son, hear the instruction of your father, and do not forsake the law of your mother;

For they will be graceful ornaments on your head, and chains about your neck.
PROVERBS 1:8–9

How can a young man cleanse his way? By taking heed according to Your word. PSALM 119:9

The rod and reproof give wisdom, but a child left to himself brings shame to his mother.
PROVERBS 29:15

But Jesus said, "Let the little children come to Me, and do not forbid them; for of such is the kingdom of heaven." MATTHEW 19:14

All your children shall be taught by the Lord, and great shall be the peace of your children. ISAIAH 54:13

Whoever loves wisdom makes his father rejoice, but a companion of harlots wastes his wealth. PROVERBS 29:3

But if any widow has children or grandchildren, let them first learn to show piety at home and to repay their parents; for this is good and acceptable before God. 1 TIMOTHY 5:4

My son, keep your father's command, and do not forsake the law of your mother.

Bind them continually upon your heart; tie them around your neck.

When you roam, they will lead you; when you sleep, they will keep you; and when you awake, they will speak with you. PROVERBS 6:20–22

Foolishness is bound up in the heart of a child, but the rod of correction will drive it far from him. PROVERBS 22:15

Do not withhold correction from a child, for if you beat him with a rod, he will not die.

You shall beat him with a rod, and deliver his soul from hell. PROVERBS 23:13–14

Marital Problems

❧ Nevertheless, because of sexual immorality, let each man have his own wife, and let each woman have her own husband.

Let the husband render to his wife the affection due her, and likewise also the wife to her husband.

The wife does not have authority over her

own body, but the husband does. And likewise the husband does not have authority over his own body, but the wife does. 2 CORINTHIANS 7:2–4

Likewise you wives, be submissive to your own husbands, that even if some do not obey the word, they, without a word, may be won by the conduct of their wives,

when they observe your chaste conduct accompanied by fear.

Do not let your beauty be that outward adorning of arranging the hair, of wearing gold, or of putting on fine apparel;

but let it be the hidden person of the heart, with the incorruptible ornament of a gentle and quiet spirit, which is very precious in the sight of God.

For in this manner, in former times, the holy women who trusted in God also adorned themselves, being submissive to their own husbands,

as Sarah obeyed Abraham, calling him lord, whose daughters you are if you do good and are not afraid with any terror.

Likewise you husbands, dwell with them with understanding, giving honor to the wife, as to the weaker vessel, and as being heirs together of the grace of life, that your prayers may not be hindered.

"For the eyes of the Lord are on the righteous, and his ears are open to their prayers; but the face of the Lord is against those who do evil." 1 PETER 3:1–7,12

Wives, submit to your own husbands, as to the Lord.

For the husband is head of the wife, as also Christ is head of the church; and He is the Savior of the body.

Therefore, just as the church is subject to Christ, so let the wives be to their own husbands in everything.

Husbands, love your wives, just as Christ also loved the church and gave Himself for it,

that He might sanctify and cleanse it with the washing of water by the word,

that He might present it to Himself a glorious church, not having spot or wrinkle or any such thing, but that it should be holy and without blemish.

So husbands ought to love their own wives as their own bodies; he who loves his wife loves himself.

For no one ever hated his own flesh, but

nourishes and cherishes it, just as the Lord does the church.

For we are members of His body, of His flesh and of His bones.

"For this reason a man shall leave his father and mother and be joined to his wife, and the two shall become one flesh."

This is a great mystery, but I speak concerning Christ and the church.

Nevertheless let each one of you in particular so love his own wife as himself, and let the wife see that she respects her husband.

EPHESIANS 5:22–33

And the Lord God said, "It is not good that man should be alone; I will make him a helper comparable to him."

Therefore a man shall leave his father and mother and be joined to his wife, and they shall become one flesh. GENESIS 2:18,24

"And if it seems evil to you to serve the Lord, choose for yourselves this day whom you will serve, whether the gods which your fathers served that were on the other side of the River, or the gods of the Amorites, in whose land you dwell. But as for me and my house, we will serve the Lord." JOSHUA 24:15

One who rules his own house well, having his children in submission with all reverence

(for if a man does not know how to rule his own house, how will he take care of the church of God?). 1 TIMOTHY 3:4–5

Since you have purified your souls in obeying the truth through the Spirit in sincere love of the brethren, love one another fervently with a pure heart. 1 PETER 1:22

Love does no harm to a neighbor; therefore love is the fulfillment of the law. ROMANS 13:10

Finally, all of you be of one mind, having compassion for one another; love as brothers, be tenderhearted, be courteous;

not returning evil for evil or reviling for reviling, but on the contrary blessing, knowing that you were called to this, that you may inherit a blessing. 1 PETER 3:8–9

Hatred stirs up strife, but love covers all sins. PROVERBS 10:12

Let all bitterness, wrath, anger, clamor, and evil speaking be put away from you, with all malice.

And be kind to one another, tenderhearted, forgiving one another, just as God in Christ also forgave you. EPHESIANS 4:31–32

Divorce

❧ "Furthermore it has been said, 'Whoever divorces his wife, let him give her a certificate of divorce.'

"But I say to you that whoever divorces his wife for any reason except sexual immorality causes her to commit adultery; and whoever marries a woman who is divorced commits adultery." MATTHEW 5:31–32

"Whoever divorces his wife and marries another commits adultery; and whoever marries her who is divorced from her husband commits adultery." LUKE 16:18

Now to the married I command, yet not I but the Lord: A wife is not to depart from her husband.

But even if she does depart, let her remain unmarried or be reconciled to her husband. And a husband is not to divorce his wife.

But to the rest I, not the Lord, say: If any brother has a wife who does not believe, and she is willing to live with him, let him not divorce her.

And a woman who has a husband who does not believe, if he is willing to live with her, let her not divorce him.

For the unbelieving husband is sanctified by the wife, and the unbelieving wife is sanctified by the husband; otherwise your children would be unclean, but now they are holy.

But if the unbeliever departs, let him depart; a brother or a sister is not under bondage in such cases. But God has called us to peace.

For how do you know, O wife, whether you will save your husband? Or how do you know, O husband, whether you will save your wife?

1 CORINTHIANS 7:10–16

"When a man takes a wife and marries her, and it happens that she finds no favor in his eyes because he has found some uncleanness in her, and he writes her a certificate of divorce, puts it in her hand, and sends her out of his house,

"when she has departed from his house, and goes and becomes another man's wife, "if the latter husband detests her and writes her a certificate of divorce, puts it in her hand, and sends her out of his house, or if the latter husband dies who took her to be his wife,

"then her former husband who divorced her must not take her back to be his wife after she has been defiled; for that is an abomination before the Lord, and you shall not bring sin on the land which the Lord your God is giving you as an inheritance." DEUTERONOMY 24:1–4

A wife is bound by law as long as her husband lives; but if her husband dies, she is at liberty to be married to whom she wishes, only in the Lord.

But she is happier if she remains as she is, according to my judgment—and I think I also have the Spirit of God. 2 CORINTHIANS 7:39–40

The Pharisees came and asked Him, "Is it lawful for a man to divorce his wife?" testing Him.

And He answered and said to them, "What did Moses command you?"

They said, "Moses permitted a man to write a certificate of divorce, and to dismiss her."

And Jesus answered and said to them,

"Because of the hardness of your heart he wrote you this precept.

"But from the beginning of the creation, God 'made them male and female.'

'For this reason a man shall leave his father and mother and be joined to his wife,

and the two shall become one flesh'; so then they are no longer two, but one flesh.

"Therefore what God has joined together, let not man separate."

And in the house His disciples asked Him again about the same matter.

So He said to them, "Whoever divorces his wife and marries another commits adultery against her.

"And if a woman divorces her husband and marries another, she commits adultery."

MARK 10:2–12

Yet you say, "For what reason?" because the Lord has been witness between you and the wife of your youth, with whom you have dealt treacherously; yet she is your companion and your wife by covenant.

But did He not make them one, having a remnant of the Spirit? And why one? He seeks godly offspring. Therefore take heed to your spirit, and let none deal treacherously with the wife of his youth.

"For the Lord God of Israel says that He hates divorce, for it covers one's garment with violence," says the Lord of hosts. "Therefore take heed to your spirit, that you do not deal treacherously." MALACHI 2:14–16

The Pharisees also came to him, testing Him, and saying to Him, "Is it lawful for a man to divorce his wife for just any reason?"

And He answered and said to them, "Have you not read that He who made them at the beginning 'made them male and female,'

"and said, 'For this reason a man shall leave his father and mother and be joined to his wife, and the two shall become one flesh'?

"So then, they are no longer two but one flesh. Therefore what God has joined together, let not man separate."

They said to Him, "Why then did Moses command to give a certificate of divorce, and to put her away?"

He said to them, "Moses, because of the hardness of your hearts, permitted you to divorce your wives, but from the beginning it was not so.

"And I say to you, whoever divorces his wife, except for sexual immorality, and marries another, commits adultery; and whoever marries her who is divorced commits adultery."

MATTHEW 19:3–9

"They say, 'If a man divorces his wife, and she goes from him and becomes another man's, may he return to her again?' Would not that land be greatly polluted? But you have played the harlot with many lovers; yet return to Me," says the Lord. JEREMIAH 3:1

Desertion

You shall no longer be termed Forsaken, nor shall your land any more be termed Desolate; but you shall be called Hephzibah, and your land Beulah; for the Lord delights in you, and your land shall be married. ISAIAH 62:4

"Can a woman forget her nursing child, and not have compassion on the son of her womb? Surely they may forget, yet I will not forget you.

"See, I have inscribed you on the palms of My hands; your walls are continually before Me." ISAIAH 49:15–16

"Be strong and of good courage, do not fear nor be afraid of them; for the Lord your God, He is the One who goes with you. He will not leave you nor forsake you." DEUTERONOMY 31:6

A father of the fatherless, a defender of widows, is God in His holy habitation.

PSALM 68:5

Do not remove the ancient landmark, nor enter the fields of the fatherless;

For their Redeemer is mighty; He will plead their cause against you. PROVERBS 23:10–11

"Leave your fatherless children, I will preserve them alive; and let your widows trust in Me." JEREMIAH 49:11

"Assyria shall not save us, we will not ride on horses, nor will we say anymore to the work of our hands, 'You are our gods.' For in You the fatherless finds mercy." HOSEA 14:3

"He administers justice for the fatherless and the widow, and loves the stranger, giving him food and clothing." DEUTERONOMY 10:18

Casting all your care upon Him, for He cares for you. 1 PETER 5:7

I have been young, and now am old; yet I have not seen the righteous forsaken, nor his descendants begging bread. PSALM 37:25

When my father and my mother forsake me, then the Lord will take care of me.

PSALM 27:10

"For the Lord your God is a merciful God, He will not forsake you nor destroy you, nor forget the covenant of your fathers which He swore to them." DEUTERONOMY 4:31

"When the poor and needy seek water, and there is none, and their tongues fail for thirst, I, the Lord, will hear them; I, the God of Israel, will not forsake them." ISAIAH 41:17

Why are you cast down, O my soul? And why are you disquieted within me? Hope in God; for I shall yet praise Him, the help of my countenance and my God. PSALM 43:5

"For the Lord will not forsake His people, for His great name's sake, because it has pleased the Lord to make you His people."
1 SAMUEL 12:22

What then shall we say to these things? If God is for us, who can be against us?
ROMANS 8:31

"Call to Me, and I will answer you, and show you great and mighty things, which you do not know." JEREMIAH 33:3

Financial Stress

And my God shall supply all your need according to His riches in glory by Christ Jesus.
PHILIPPIANS 4:19

"Therefore do not worry, saying, 'What shall we eat?' or 'What shall we drink?' or 'What shall we wear?'

"For after all these things the Gentiles seek. For your heavenly Father knows that you need all these things.

"But seek first the kingdom of God and His righteousness, and all these things shall be added to you." MATTHEW 6:31–33

"And all these blessings shall come upon you and overtake you, because you obey the voice of the Lord your God:

"Blessed shall you be in the city, and blessed shall you be in the country.

"Blessed shall be the fruit of your body, the produce of your ground and the increase of your herds, the increase of your cattle and the offspring of your flocks.

"Blessed shall be your basket and your kneading bowl.

"Blessed shall you be when you come in, and blessed shall you be when you go out.

"The Lord will cause your enemies who rise against you to be defeated before your face; they shall come out against you one way and flee before you seven ways.

"The Lord will command the blessing on you in your storehouses and in all to which you set your hand, and He will bless you in the land which the Lord your God is giving you."

DEUTERONOMY 28:2–8

"Bring all the tithes into the storehouse, that there may be food in My house, and prove Me now in this," says the Lord of hosts, "if I will not open for you the windows of heaven and pour out for you such blessing that there will not be room enough to receive it.

"And I will rebuke the devourer for your sakes, so that he will not destroy the fruit of your ground, nor shall the vine fail to bear fruit for you in the field," says the Lord of hosts;

"And all nations will call you blessed, for you will be a delightful land," says the Lord of hosts. MALACHI 3:10–12

But this I say: He who sows sparingly will also reap sparingly, and he who sows bountifully will also reap bountifully.

So let each one give as he purposes in his heart, not grudgingly or of necessity; for God loves a cheerful giver.

And God is able to make all grace abound toward you, that you, always having all sufficiency in all things, have an abundance for every good work. 2 CORINTHIANS 9:6–8

"Give, and it will be given to you: good measure, pressed down, shaken together, and running over will be put into your bosom. For with the same measure that you use, it will be measured back to you." LUKE 6:38

"And the Lord will grant you plenty of goods, in the fruit of your body, in the increase of your livestock, and in the produce of your ground, in the land of which the Lord swore to your fathers to give you.

"The Lord will open to you His good treasure, the heavens, to give the rain to your land in its season, and to bless all the work of your hand. You shall lend to many nations, but you shall not borrow.

"And the Lord will make you the head and not the tail; you shall be above only, and not be beneath, if you heed the commandments of the Lord your God, which I command you today, and are careful to observe them."

DEUTERONOMY 28:11–13

"And everyone who has left houses or brothers or sisters or father or mother or wife or children or lands, for My name's sake, shall receive a hundredfold, and inherit everlasting life." MATTHEW 19:29

"This Book of the Law shall not depart from your mouth, but you shall meditate in it day and night, that you may observe to do according to all that is written in it. For then you will make your way prosperous, and then you will have good success." JOSHUA 1:8

A good man leaves an inheritance to his children's children, but the wealth of the sinner is stored up for the righteous. PROVERBS 13:22

But godliness with contentment is great gain.

Command those who are rich in this present age not to be haughty, nor to trust in uncertain riches but in the living God, who gives us richly all things to enjoy. 1 TIMOTHY 6:6,17

He who did not spare His own Son, but delivered Him up for us all, how shall He not with Him also freely give us all things?

ROMANS 8:32

Oh, fear the Lord, you His saints! There is no want to those who fear Him.

The young lions lack and suffer hunger; but those who seek the Lord shall not lack any good thing. PSALM 34:9–10

I will abundantly bless her provision; I will satisfy her poor with bread. PSALM 132:15

Therefore let no one glory in men. For all things are yours:

whether Paul or Apollos or Cephas, or the world or life or death, or things present or things to come—all are yours.

1 CORINTHIANS 3:21–22

Who is the man who desires life, and loves many days, that he may see good?

Depart from evil, and do good; seek peace, and pursue it. PSALM 34:12,14

For the Lord God is a sun and shield; the Lord will give grace and glory; no good thing will He withhold from those who walk uprightly.

PSALM 84:11

"Say to the righteous that it shall be well with them, for they shall eat the fruit of their doings." ISAIAH 3:10

Surely goodness and mercy shall follow me all the days of my life; and I will dwell in the house of the Lord forever. PSALM 23:6

The Lord is my shepherd; I shall not want.
You prepare a table before me in the presence of my enemies; You anoint my head with oil; My cup runs over. PSALM 23:1,5

Though a sinner does evil a hundred times, and his days are prolonged, yet I surely know that it will be well with those who fear God, who fear before Him. ECCLESIASTES 8:12

PROMISES FOR VARIOUS RELATIONSHIPS

Marriage

He who finds a wife finds a good thing, and obtains favor from the Lord. PROVERBS 18:22

And the Lord God said, "It is not good that man should be alone; I will make him a helper comparable to him."

Therefore a man shall leave his father and mother and be joined to his wife, and they shall become one flesh. GENESIS 2:18,24

Who can find a virtuous wife? For her worth is far above rubies.

The heart of her husband safely trusts her; so he will have no lack of gain.

She does him good and not evil all the days of her life. PROVERBS 31:10–12

"And said, 'For this reason a man shall leave his father and mother and be joined to his wife, and the two shall become one flesh'?

"So then, they are no longer two but one flesh. Therefore what God has joined together, let not man separate." MATTHEW 19:5–6

Take wives and beget sons and daughters; and take wives for your sons and give your daughters to husbands, so that they may bear sons and daughters—that you may be increased there, and not diminished.

JEREMIAH 29:6

Therefore I desire that the younger widows marry, bear children, manage the house, give no opportunity to the adversary to speak reproachfully. 1 TIMOTHY 5:14

Now concerning the things of which you wrote to me: It is good for a man not to touch a woman.

Nevertheless, because of sexual immorality, let each man have his own wife, and let each woman have her own husband.

Let the husband render to his wife the affection due her, and likewise also the wife to her husband.

The wife does not have authority over her own body, but the husband does. And likewise the husband does not have authority over his own body, but the wife does.

Do not deprive one another except with consent for a time, that you may give yourselves to fasting and prayer; and come together again so that Satan does not tempt you because of your lack of self-control.

1 CORINTHIANS 7:1–5

Marriage is honorable among all, and the bed undefiled; but fornicators and adulterers God will judge. HEBREWS 13:4

An excellent wife is the crown of her husband, but she who causes shame is like rottenness in his bones. PROVERBS 12:4

But even if she does depart, let her remain unmarried or be reconciled to her husband. And a husband is not to divorce his wife.

But to the rest I, not the Lord, say: If any brother has a wife who does not believe, and she is willing to live with him, let him not divorce her. 1 CORINTHIANS 7:11–12

Charm is deceitful and beauty is vain, but a woman who fears the Lord, she shall be praised.

Give her of the fruit of her hands, and let her own works praise her in the gates.

PROVERBS 31:30–31

"For this reason a man shall leave his father and mother and be joined to his wife, and the two shall become one flesh."

This is a great mystery, but I speak concerning Christ and the church.

Nevertheless let each one of you in particular so love his own wife as himself, and let the wife see that she respects her husband.

EPHESIANS 5:31–33

"But from the beginning of the creation, God 'made them male and female.'

'For this reason a man shall leave his father and mother and be joined to his wife,

and the two shall become one flesh'; so then they are no longer two, but one flesh.

"Therefore what God has joined together, let not man separate." MARK 10:6–9

Your wife shall be like a fruitful vine in the very heart of your house, your children like olive plants all around your table.

Behold, thus shall the man be blessed who fears the Lord.

The Lord bless you out of Zion, and may you see the good of Jerusalem all the days of your life.

Yes, may you see your children's children.
Peace be upon Israel! PSALM 128:3–6

"You shall teach them to your children, speaking of them when you sit in your house, when you walk by the way, when you lie down, and when you rise up.

"And you shall write them on the doorposts of your house and on your gates,

"that your days and days of your children may be multiplied in the land of which the Lord swore to your fathers to give them, like the days of the heavens above the earth."

DEUTERONOMY 11:19–21

Likewise you wives, be submissive to your own husbands, that even if some do not obey the word, they, without a word, may be won by the conduct of their wives.

Likewise you husbands, dwell with them with understanding, giving honor to the wife, as to the weaker vessel, and as being heirs together of the grace of life, that your prayers may not be hindered. 1 PETER 3:1,7

Hatred stirs up strife, but love covers all sins. PROVERBS 10:12

For this is the will of God, your sanctification: that you should abstain from sexual immorality;

that each of you should know how to possess his own vessel in sanctification and honor,

not in passion of lust, like the Gentiles who do not know God;

that no one should take advantage of and defraud his brother in this matter, because the Lord is the avenger of all such, as we also forewarned you and testified.

1 THESSALONIANS 4:3–6

Business

❧ Beloved, I pray that you may prosper in all things and be in health, just as your soul prospers. 3 JOHN 1:2

"And you shall remember the Lord your God, for it is He who gives you power to get wealth, that He may establish His covenant which He swore to your fathers, as it is this day." DEUTERONOMY 8:18

Trust in the Lord with all your heart, and lean not on your own understanding;

In all your ways acknowledge Him, and He shall direct your paths.

Do not be wise in your own eyes; fear the Lord and depart from evil.

It will be health to your flesh, and strength to your bones.

Honor the Lord with your possessions, and with the firstfruits of all your increase;

So your barns will be filled with plenty, and your vats will overflow with new wine.

PROVERBS 3:5–10

"Now it shall come to pass, if you diligently obey the voice of the Lord your God, to observe carefully all His commandments which I command you today, that the Lord your God will set you high above all nations of the earth.

"And all these blessings shall come upon you and overtake you, because you obey the voice of the Lord your God:

"Blessed shall you be in the city, and blessed shall you be in the country.

"Blessed shall be the fruit of your body, the produce of your ground and the increase of your herds, the increase of your cattle and the offspring of your flocks.

"Blessed shall be your basket and your kneading bowl.

"Blessed shall you be when you come in, and blessed shall you be when you go out."

DEUTERONOMY 28:1–6

Blessed is the man who walks not in the counsel of the ungodly, nor stands in the path of sinners, nor sits in the seat of the scornful;

But his delight is in the law of the Lord, and in His law he meditates day and night.

He shall be like a tree planted by the rivers of water, that brings forth its fruit in its season, whose leaf also shall not wither; and whatever he does shall prosper. PSALM 1:1–3

Commit your works to the Lord, and your thoughts will be established. PROVERBS 16:3

Through wisdom a house is built, and by understanding it is established;

By knowledge the rooms are filled with all precious and pleasant riches. PROVERBS 24:3–4

If they obey and serve Him, they shall spend their days in prosperity, and their years in pleasures. JOB 36:11

"The Lord will command the blessing on you in your storehouses and in all to which you set your hand, and He will bless you in the land which the Lord your God is giving you."

DEUTERONOMY 28:8

Masters, give your servants what is just and fair, knowing that you also have a Master in heaven. COLOSSIANS 4:1

"And the Lord will grant you plenty of goods, in the fruit of your body, in the increase of your livestock, and in the produce of your ground, in the land of which the Lord swore to your fathers to give you.

"The Lord will open to you His good treasure, the heavens, to give the rain to your land in its season, and to bless all the work of your hand. You shall lend to many nations, but you shall not borrow.

"And the Lord will make you the head and not the tail; you shall be above only, and not be beneath, if you heed the commandments of the

Lord your God, which I command you today, and are careful to observe them."

DEUTERONOMY 28:11–13

"But seek first the kingdom of God and His righteousness, and all these things shall be added to you." MATTHEW 6:33

"I go the way of all the earth; be strong, therefore, and prove yourself a man.

"And keep the charge of the Lord your God: to walk in His ways, to keep His statutes, His commandments, His judgments, and His testimonies, as it is written in the Law of Moses, that you may prosper in all that you do and wherever you turn." 1 KINGS 2:2–3

"Then you will prosper, if you take care to fulfill the statutes and judgments with which the Lord charged Moses concerning Israel. Be strong and of good courage; do not fear nor be dismayed." 1 CHRONICLES 22:13

"Then I will give you the rain for your land in its season, the early rain and the latter rain, that you may gather in your grain, your new wine, and your oil.

"And I will send grass in your fields for your livestock, that you may eat and be filled."
DEUTERONOMY 11:14–15

When you eat the labor of your hands, you shall be happy, and it shall be well with you.
PSALM 128:2

Then you will lay your gold in the dust, and the gold of Ophir among the stones of the brooks.

Yes, the Almighty will be your gold and your precious silver. JOB 22:24–25

Then He will give the rain for your seed with which you sow the ground, and bread of the increase of the earth; it will be fat and plenteous. In that day your cattle will feed in large pastures. ISAIAH 30:23

He also blesses them, and they multiply greatly; and He does not let their cattle decrease. PSALM 107:38

They shall build houses and inhabit them; they shall plant vineyards and eat their fruit.

They shall not build and another inhabit;

they shall not plant and another eat; for as the days of a tree, so shall be the days of My people, and My elect shall long enjoy the work of their hands.

They shall not labor in vain, nor bring forth children for trouble; for they shall be the descendants of the blessed of the Lord, and their offspring with them. ISAIAH 65:21–23

Wealth and riches will be in his house, and his righteousness endures forever. PSALM 112:3

Riches and honor are with me, enduring riches and righteousness.

My fruit is better than gold, yes, than fine gold, and my revenue than choice silver.

PROVERBS 8:18–19

Social

"You are the light of the world. A city that is set on a hill cannot be hidden.

"Nor do they light a lamp and put it under a basket, but on a lampstand, and it gives light to all who are in the house.

"Let your light so shine before men, that

they may see your good works and glorify your Father in heaven." MATTHEW 5:14–16

"And He will set the sheep on His right hand, but the goats on the left.

"Then the King will say to those on His right hand, 'Come, you blessed of My Father, inherit the kingdom prepared for you from the foundation of the world:

'for I was hungry and you gave Me food; I was thirsty and you gave Me drink; I was a stranger and you took Me in;

'I was naked and you clothed Me; I was sick and you visited Me; I was in prison and you came to Me.'

"Then the righteous will answer Him, saying, 'Lord, when did we see You hungry and feed You, or thirsty and give You drink?

'When did we see You a stranger and take You in, or naked and clothe You?

'Or when did we see You sick, or in prison, and come to You?'

"And the King will answer and say to them, 'Assuredly, I say to you, inasmuch as you did it to one of the least of these My brethren, you did it to Me.'" MATTHEW 25:33–40

Let love be without hypocrisy. Abhor what is evil. Cling to what is good.

Be kindly affectionate to one another with brotherly love, in honor giving preference to one another;

not lagging in diligence, fervent in spirit, serving the Lord;

rejoicing in hope, patient in tribulation, continuing steadfastly in prayer;

distributing to the needs of the saints, given to hospitality.

Bless those who persecute you; bless and do not curse.

Rejoice with those who rejoice, and weep with those who weep. ROMANS 12:9–15

"A new commandment I give to you, that you love one another; as I have loved you, that you also love one another.

"By this all will know that you are My disciples, if you have love for one another."

JOHN 13:34–35

"Go therefore and make disciples of all the nations, baptizing them in the name of the Father and of the Son and of the Holy Spirit,

"teaching them to observe all things that I

have commanded you; and lo, I am with you always, even to the end of the age." Amen.

MATTHEW 28:19–20

For none of us lives to himself, and no one dies to himself.

For if we live, we live to the Lord; and if we die, we die to the Lord. Therefore, whether we live or die, we are the Lord's. ROMANS 14:7–8

And you, masters, do the same things to them, giving up threatening, knowing that your own Master also is in heaven, and there is no partiality with Him. EPHESIANS 6:9

"Woe to him who builds his house by unrighteousness and his chambers by injustice, who uses his neighbor's service without wages and gives him nothing for his work."

JEREMIAH 22:13

We then who are strong ought to bear with the scruples of the weak, and not to please ourselves.

Let each of us please his neighbor for his good, leading to edification.

For even Christ did not please Himself; but

as it is written, "The reproaches of those who reproached You fell on Me."

For whatever things were written before were written for our learning, that we through the patience and comfort of the Scriptures might have hope.

Now may the God of patience and comfort grant you to be like-minded toward one another, according to Christ Jesus,

that you may with one mind and one mouth glorify the God and Father of our Lord Jesus Christ. ROMANS 15:1–6

"You are the salt of the earth; but if the salt loses its flavor, how shall it be seasoned? It is then good for nothing but to be thrown out and trampled under foot by men." MATTHEW 5:13

Therefore do not let your good be spoken of as evil;

for the kingdom of God is not food and drink, but righteousness and peace and joy in the Holy Spirit.

For he who serves Christ in these things is acceptable to God and approved by men.

Therefore let us pursue the things which make for peace and the things by which one may edify another.

Do not destroy the work of God for the sake of food. All things indeed are pure, but it is evil for the man who eats with offense.

It is good neither to eat meat nor drink wine nor do anything by which your brother stumbles or is offended or is made weak.

ROMANS 14:16–21

"You shall not defraud your neighbor, nor rob him. The wages of him who is hired shall not remain with you all night until morning."

LEVITICUS 19:13

Be of the same mind toward one another. Do not set your mind on high things, but associate with the humble. Do not be wise in your own opinion.

Repay no one evil for evil. Have regard for good things in the sight of all men.

If it is possible, as much as depends on you, live peaceably with all men.

Beloved, do not avenge yourselves, but rather give place to wrath; for it is written, "Vengeance is Mine, I will repay," says the Lord.

"Therefore if your enemy hungers, feed him; if he thirsts, give him a drink; for in so doing you will heap coals of fire on his head."

Do not be overcome by evil, but overcome evil with good. ROMANS 12:16–21

Owe no one anything except to love one another, for he who loves another has fulfilled the law.

For the commandments, "You shall not commit adultery," "You shall not murder," "You shall not steal," "You shall not bear false witness," "You shall not covet," and if there is any other commandment, are all summed up in this saying, namely, "You shall love your neighbor as yourself."

Love does no harm to a neighbor; therefore love is the fulfillment of the law. ROMANS 13:8–10

Therefore, as the elect of God, holy and beloved, put on tender mercies, kindness, humbleness of mind, meekness, longsuffering;

bearing with one another, and forgiving one another, if anyone has a complaint against another; even as Christ forgave you, so you also must do.

But above all these things put on love, which is the bond of perfection.

And let the peace of God rule in your hearts, to which also you were called in one body; and be thankful. COLOSSIANS 3:12–15

Church

❧ And Simon Peter answered and said, "You are the Christ, the Son of the living God."

Jesus answered and said to him, "Blessed are you, Simon Bar-Jonah, for flesh and blood has not revealed this to you, but My Father who is in heaven.

"And I also say to you that you are Peter, and on this rock I will build My church, and the gates of Hades shall not prevail against it.

"And I will give you the keys of the kingdom of heaven, and whatever you bind on earth will be bound in heaven, and whatever you loose on earth will be loosed in heaven." MATTHEW 16:16–19

Now the multitude of those who believed were of one heart and one soul; neither did anyone say that any of the things he possessed was his own, but they had all things in common.

And with great power the apostles gave witness to the resurrection of the Lord Jesus. And great grace was upon them all.

Nor was there anyone among them who lacked; for all who were possessors of lands or houses sold them, and brought the proceeds of the things that were sold, and laid them at the apostles' feet; and they distributed to each as anyone had need.

ACTS 4:32–35

For the husband is head of the wife, as also Christ is head of the church; and He is the Savior of the body.

Therefore, just as the church is subject to Christ, so let the wives be to their own husbands in everything.

Husbands, love your wives, just as Christ also loved the church and gave Himself for it,

that He might sanctify and cleanse it with the washing of water by the word,

that He might present it to Himself a glorious church, not having spot or wrinkle or any such thing, but that it should be holy and without blemish. EPHESIANS 5:23–27

That in the dispensation of the fullness of the times He might gather together in one all things in Christ, both which are in heaven and which are on earth—in Him.

And He put all things under His feet, and gave Him to be head over all things to the church,

which is His body, the fullness of Him who fills all in all. EPHESIANS 1:10,22–23

But Jesus called them to Himself and said, "You know that the rulers of the Gentiles lord it over them, and those who are great exercise authority over them.

"Yet it shall not be so among you; but whoever desires to become great among you, let him be your servant." MATTHEW 20:25–26

"No longer do I call you servants, for a servant does not know what his master is doing; but I have called you friends, for all things that I heard from My Father I have made known to you.

"You did not choose Me, but I chose you and appointed you that you should go and bear fruit, and that your fruit should remain, that whatever you ask the Father in My name He may give you." JOHN 15:15–16

These all continued with one accord in prayer and supplication, with the women and Mary the mother of Jesus, and with His brothers.

Now when the Day of Pentecost had fully come, they were all with one accord in one place. ACTS 1:14; 2:1

For no one ever hated his own flesh, but nourishes and cherishes it, just as the Lord does the church.

For we are members of His body, of His flesh and of His bones. EPHESIANS 5:29–30

So continuing daily with one accord in the temple, and breaking bread from house to house, they ate their food with gladness and simplicity of heart,

praising God and having favor with all the people. And the Lord added to the church daily those who were being saved. ACTS 2:46–47

And He Himself gave some to be apostles, some prophets, some evangelists, and some pastors and teachers,

for the equipping of the saints for the work of ministry, for the edifying of the body of Christ,

till we all come to the unity of the faith and the knowledge of the Son of God, to a perfect man, to the measure of the stature of the fullness of Christ;

that we should no longer be children, tossed to and fro and carried about with every wind of doctrine, by the trickery of men, in the cunning craftiness by which they lie in wait to deceive,

but, speaking the truth in love, may grow up in all things into Him who is the head—Christ—

from whom the whole body, joined and knit together by what every joint supplies, according to the effective working by which every part does its share, causes growth of the body for the edifying of itself in love. EPHESIANS 4:11–16

And a servant of the Lord must not quarrel but be gentle to all, able to teach, patient,

in humility correcting those who are in opposition, if God perhaps will grant them repentance, so that they may know the truth,

and that they may come to their senses and escape the snare of the devil, having been taken captive by him to do his will. 2 TIMOTHY 2:24–26

"A new commandment I give to you, that you love one another; as I have loved you, that you also love one another." JOHN 13:34

Then the churches throughout all Judea, Galilee, and Samaria had peace and were edified. And walking in the fear of the Lord and in the comfort of the Holy Spirit, they were multiplied. ACTS 9:31

Now to Him who is able to do exceedingly abundantly above all that we ask or think, according to the power that works in us,

to Him be glory in the church by Christ Jesus throughout all ages, world without end. Amen. EPHESIANS 3:20–21

Let the word of Christ dwell in you richly in all wisdom, teaching and admonishing one another in psalms and hymns and spiritual songs, singing with grace in your hearts to the Lord.

And whatever you do in word or deed, do all in the name of the Lord Jesus, giving thanks to God the Father through Him.

COLOSSIANS 3:16–17

Government

❧ Therefore submit yourselves to every ordinance of man for the Lord's sake, whether to the king as supreme,

or to governors, as to those who are sent by him for the punishment of evildoers and for the praise of those who do good.

For this is the will of God, that by doing good you may put to silence the ignorance of foolish men. 1 PETER 2:13–15

Let every soul be subject to the governing authorities. For there is no authority except from God, and the authorities that exist are appointed by God.

Therefore whoever resists the authority resists the ordinance of God, and those who resist will bring judgment on themselves.

For rulers are not a terror to good works, but to evil. Do you want to be unafraid of the authority? Do what is good, and you will have praise from the same.

For he is God's minister to you for good. But if you do evil, be afraid; for he does not bear the sword in vain; for he is God's minister, an avenger to execute wrath on him who practices evil.

Therefore you must be subject, not only because of wrath but also for conscience' sake.

For because of this you also pay taxes, for they are God's ministers attending continually to this very thing.

Render therefore to all their due: taxes to whom taxes are due, customs to whom customs, fear to whom fear, honor to whom honor. ROMANS 13:1-7

Remind them to be subject to rulers and authorities, to obey, to be ready for every good work,

to speak evil of no one, to be peaceable, gentle, showing all humility to all men.

TITUS 3:1–2

Then Pilate said to Him, "Are You not speaking to me? Do You not know that I have power to crucify You, and power to release You?"

Jesus answered, "You could have no power at all against Me unless it had been given you from above. Therefore the one who delivered Me to you has the greater sin." JOHN 19:10–11

Daniel answered and said: "Blessed be the name of God forever and ever, for wisdom and might are His.

"And He changes the times and the seasons; He removes kings and raises up kings; He gives wisdom to the wise and knowledge to those who have understanding."

DANIEL 2:20–21

It is an abomination for kings to commit wickedness, for a throne is established by righteousness. PROVERBS 16:12

Mercy and truth preserve the king, and by lovingkindness he upholds his throne.

PROVERBS 20:28

The king who judges the poor with truth, his throne will be established forever.

PROVERBS 29:14

"'This decision is by the decree of the watchers, and the sentence by the word of the holy ones, in order that the living may know that the Most High rules in the kingdom of men, gives it to whomever He will, and sets over it the lowest of men.'" DANIEL 4:17

Then Samuel called the people together to the Lord at Mizpah,

and said to the children of Israel, "Thus says the Lord God of Israel: 'I brought up Israel out of Egypt, and delivered you from the hand of the Egyptians and from the hand of all kingdoms and from those who oppressed you.'

"But you have today rejected your God, who

Himself saved you out of all your adversities and your tribulations; and you have said to Him, 'No, but set a king over us!' Now therefore, present yourselves before the Lord by your tribes and by your clans." 1 SAMUEL 10:17–19

"Now therefore, here is the king whom you have chosen and whom you have desired. And take note, the Lord has set a king over you.

"If you fear the Lord and serve Him and obey His voice, and do not rebel against the commandment of the Lord, then both you and the king who reigns over you will continue following the Lord your God.

"However, if you do not obey the voice of the Lord, but rebel against the commandment of the Lord, then the hand of the Lord will be against you, as it was against your fathers."

1 SAMUEL 12:13–15

Unsaved Loved Ones

"Even so it is not the will of your Father who is in heaven that one of these little ones should perish." MATTHEW 18:14

The Lord is not slack concerning His promise, as some count slackness, but is longsuffering toward us, not willing that any should perish but that all should come to repentance. 2 PETER 3:9

Train up a child in the way he should go, and when he is old he will not depart from it.

PROVERBS 22:6

Likewise you wives, be submissive to your own husbands, that even if some do not obey the word, they, without a word, may be won by the conduct of their wives,

when they observe your chaste conduct accompanied by fear. 1 PETER 3:1–2

But even if you should suffer for righteousness' sake, you are blessed. "And do not be afraid of their threats, nor be troubled."

But sanctify the Lord God in your hearts, and always be ready to give a defense to everyone who asks you a reason for the hope that is in you, with meekness and fear;

having a good conscience, that when they defame you as evildoers, those who revile your good conduct in Christ may be ashamed.

1 PETER 3:14–16

So they said, "Believe on the Lord Jesus Christ, and you will be saved, you and your household." ACTS 16:31

"Who will tell you words by which you and all your household will be saved." ACTS 11:14

And a woman who has a husband who does not believe, if he is willing to live with her, let her not divorce him.

For the unbelieving husband is sanctified by the wife, and the unbelieving wife is sanctified by the husband; otherwise your children would be unclean, but now they are holy.

But if the unbeliever departs, let him depart; a brother or a sister is not under bondage in such cases. But God has called us to peace.

For how do you know, O wife, whether you will save your husband? Or how do you know, O husband, whether you will save your wife?

1 CORINTHIANS 7:13–16

For I will pour water on him who is thirsty, and floods on the dry ground; I will pour My Spirit on your descendants, and My blessing on your offspring. ISAIAH 44:3

"Nevertheless I tell you the truth. It is to your advantage that I go away; for if I do not go away, the Helper will not come to you; but if I depart, I will send Him to you.

"And when He has come, He will convict the world of sin, and of righteousness, and of judgment." JOHN 16:7–8

Having your conduct honorable among the Gentiles, that when they speak against you as evildoers, they may, by your good works which they observe, glorify God in the day of visitation.

Therefore submit yourselves to every ordinance of man for the Lord's sake, whether to the king as supreme,

or to governors, as to those who are sent by him for the punishment of evildoers and for the praise of those who do good.

For this is the will of God, that by doing good you may put to silence the ignorance of foolish men. 1 PETER 2:12–15

"You are the salt of the earth; but if the salt loses its flavor, how shall it be seasoned? It is then good for nothing but to be thrown out and trampled under foot by men." MATTHEW 5:13

"You are the light of the world. A city that is set on a hill cannot be hidden.

"Nor do they light a lamp and put it under a basket, but on a lampstand, and it gives light to all who are in the house.

"Let your light so shine before men, that they may see your good works and glorify your Father in heaven." MATTHEW 5:14–16

If anyone speaks, let him speak as the oracles of God. If anyone ministers, let him do it as with the ability which God supplies, that in all things God may be glorified through Jesus Christ, to whom belong the glory and the dominion forever and ever. Amen. 1 PETER 4:11

If you are reproached for the name of Christ, blessed are you, for the Spirit of glory and of God rests upon you. On their part He is blasphemed, but on your part He is glorified.
1 PETER 4:14

"By this all will know that you are My disciples, if you have love for one another."
JOHN 13:35

The Elderly

O God, You have taught me from my youth; and to this day I declare Your wondrous works.

Now also when I am old and gray-headed, O God, do not forsake me, until I declare Your strength to this generation, Your power to everyone who is to come. PSALM 71:17–18

With long life I will satisfy him, and show him My salvation. PSALM 91:16

Even to your old age, I am He, and even to gray hairs I will carry you! I have made, and I will bear; even I will carry, and will deliver you.

ISAIAH 46:4

The silver-haired head is a crown of glory, if it is found in the way of righteousness.

PROVERBS 16:31

They shall still bear fruit in old age; they shall be fresh and flourishing. PSALM 92:14

The glory of young men is their strength, and the splendor of old men is their gray head.

PROVERBS 20:29

For length of days and long life and peace they will add to you.

Length of days is in her right hand, in her left hand riches and honor. PROVERBS 3:2,16

Surely goodness and mercy shall follow me all the days of my life; and I will dwell in the house of the Lord forever. PSALM 23:6

I have been young, and now am old; yet I have not seen the righteous forsaken, nor his descendants begging bread. PSALM 37:25

Let your conduct be without covetousness, and be content with such things as you have. For He Himself has said, "I will never leave you nor forsake you." HEBREWS 13:5

The Lord shall preserve you from all evil; He shall preserve your soul.

The Lord shall preserve your going out and your coming in from this time forth, and even forevermore. PSALM 121:7–8

The Lord preserves all who love Him, but all the wicked He will destroy. PSALM 145:20

"You shall walk in all the ways which the Lord your God has commanded you, that you may live and that it may be well with you, and that you may prolong your days in the land which you shall possess." DEUTERONOMY 5:33

"That you may fear the Lord your God, to keep all His statutes and His commandments which I command you, you and your son and your grandson, all the days of your life, and that your days may be prolonged." DEUTERONOMY 6:2

I have set the Lord always before me; because He is at my right hand I shall not be moved. PSALM 16:8

You shall come to the grave at a full age, as a sheaf of grain ripens in its season. JOB 5:26

Who is the man who desires life, and loves many days, that he may see good?

Depart from evil, and do good; seek peace, and pursue it. PSALM 34:12,14

For by me your days will be multiplied, and years of life will be added to you. PROVERBS 9:11

Of Benjamin he said: "The beloved of the Lord shall dwell in safety by Him, who shelters him all the day long; and he shall dwell between His shoulders." DEUTERONOMY 33:12

The fear of the Lord prolongs days, but the years of the wicked will be shortened.
PROVERBS 10:27

Satan

And the God of peace will crush Satan under your feet shortly. The grace of our Lord Jesus Christ be with you. Amen. ROMANS 16:20

Finally, my brethren, be strong in the Lord and in the power of His might.

Put on the whole armor of God, that you may be able to stand against the wiles of the devil.

For we do not wrestle against flesh and blood, but against principalities, against powers, against the rulers of the darkness of this age, against spiritual hosts of wickedness in the heavenly places. EPHESIANS 6:10–12

Therefore submit to God. Resist the devil and he will flee from you. JAMES 4:7

Be sober, be vigilant; because your adversary the devil walks about like a roaring lion, seeking whom he may devour.

Resist him, steadfast in the faith, knowing that the same sufferings are experienced by your brotherhood in the world. 1 PETER 5:8–9

But we see Jesus, who was made a little lower than the angels, for the suffering of death crowned with glory and honor, that He, by the grace of God, might taste death for everyone.

Inasmuch then as the children have partaken of flesh and blood, He Himself likewise shared in the same, that through death He might destroy him who had the power of death, that is, the devil,

and release those who through fear of death were all their lifetime subject to bondage.

HEBREWS 2:9,14–15

Therefore take up the whole armor of God, that you may be able to withstand in the evil day, and having done all, to stand.

Stand therefore, having girded your waist with truth, having put on the breastplate of righteousness,

and having shod your feet with the preparation of the gospel of peace;

above all, taking the shield of faith with which you will be able to quench all the fiery darts of the wicked one.

And take the helmet of salvation, and the sword of the Spirit, which is the word of God;

praying always with all prayer and supplication in the Spirit, being watchful to this end with all perseverance and supplication for all the saints. EPHESIANS 6:13–18

He has delivered us from the power of darkness and translated us into the kingdom of the Son of His love. COLOSSIANS 1:13

And you are complete in Him, who is the head of all principality and power.

Having disarmed principalities and powers, He made a public spectacle of them, triumphing over them in it. COLOSSIANS 2:10,15

Beloved, do not believe every spirit, but test the spirits, whether they are of God; because many false prophets have gone out into the world.

By this you know the Spirit of God: Every spirit that confesses that Jesus Christ has come in the flesh is of God, and every spirit that does not confess that Jesus Christ has come in the flesh is not of God.

And this is the spirit of the Antichrist, which you have heard was coming, and is now already in the world.

You are of God, little children, and have overcome them, because He who is in you is greater than he who is in the world. 1 JOHN 4:1–4

"And they overcame him by the blood of the Lamb and by the word of their testimony, and they did not love their lives to the death."

REVELATION 12:11

"How you are fallen from heaven, O Lucifer, son of the morning! How you are cut down to the ground, you who weakened the nations!

"For you have said in your heart: 'I will ascend into heaven, I will exalt my throne above the stars of God; I will also sit on the mount of the congregation on the farthest sides of the north;

'I will ascend above the heights of the clouds, I will be like the Most High.'

"Yet you shall be brought down to Sheol, to the lowest depths of the Pit." ISAIAH 14:12–15

He who sins is of the devil, for the devil has sinned from the beginning. For this purpose the Son of God was manifested, that He might destroy the works of the devil. 1 JOHN 3:8

For though we walk in the flesh, we do not war according to the flesh.

For the weapons of our warfare are not carnal but mighty in God for pulling down strongholds,

casting down arguments and every high thing that exalts itself against the knowledge of God, bringing every thought into captivity to the obedience of Christ. 2 CORINTHIANS 10:3–5

"But if I cast out demons by the Spirit of God, surely the kingdom of God has come upon you.

"Or else how can one enter a strong man's house and plunder his goods, unless he first binds the strong man? And then he will plunder his house." MATTHEW 12:28–29

Then the seventy returned with joy, saying, "Lord, even the demons are subject to us in Your name."

And He said to them, "I saw Satan fall like lightning from heaven.

"Behold, I give you the authority to trample on serpents and scorpions, and over all the power of the enemy, and nothing shall by any means hurt you." LUKE 10:17–19

"And these signs will follow those who believe: In My name they will cast out demons; they will speak with new tongues;

"they will take up serpents; and if they drink anything deadly, it will by no means hurt them; they will lay hands on the sick, and they will recover." MARK 16:17–18

So shall they fear the name of the Lord from the west, and His glory from the rising of the sun; when the enemy comes in like a flood, the Spirit of the Lord will lift up a standard against him. ISAIAH 59:19

And then the lawless one will be revealed, whom the Lord will consume with the breath of His mouth and destroy with the brightness of His coming. 2 THESSALONIANS 2:8

PROMISES OF THE TRIUMPH OF GOOD

God's Faithfulness

❧ If we are faithless, He remains faithful; He cannot deny Himself.

Nevertheless the solid foundation of God stands, having this seal: "The Lord knows those who are His," and, "Let everyone who names the name of Christ depart from iniquity."

2 TIMOTHY 2:13,19

God is faithful, by whom you were called into the fellowship of His Son, Jesus Christ our Lord. 1 CORINTHIANS 1:9

He who calls you is faithful, who also will do it. 1 THESSALONIANS 5:24

Your mercy, O Lord, is in the heavens, and Your faithfulness reaches to the clouds.

PSALM 36:5

Therefore justice is far from us, nor does righteousness overtake us; we look for light, but there is darkness! For brightness, but we walk in blackness!

We grope for the wall like the blind, and we grope as if we had no eyes; we stumble at noonday as at twilight; we are as dead men in desolate places. ISAIAH 59:9–10

"Blessed be the Lord, who has given rest to His people Israel, according to all that He promised. There has not failed one word of all His good promise, which He promised through His servant Moses." 1 KINGS 8:56

For this is God, our God forever and ever; He will be our guide even to death. PSALM 48:14

"Fear not, for I am with you; be not dismayed, for I am your God. I will strengthen you, yes, I will help you, I will uphold you with My righteous right hand." ISAIAH 41:10

My flesh and my heart fail; but God is the strength of my heart and my portion forever.
PSALM 73:26

"And the Lord, He is the one who goes before you. He will be with you, He will not leave you nor forsake you; do not fear nor be dismayed." DEUTERONOMY 31:8

Then you shall know that I am in the midst of Israel, and that I am the Lord your God and there is no other. My people shall never be put to shame. JOEL 2:27

"For this is like the waters of Noah to Me; for as I have sworn that the waters of Noah would no longer cover the earth, so have I sworn that I would not be angry with you, nor rebuke you." ISAIAH 54:9

"Behold, I am with you and will keep you wherever you go, and will bring you back to this land; for I will not leave you until I have done what I have spoken to you." GENESIS 28:15

"But because the Lord loves you, and because He would keep the oath which He swore to your fathers, the Lord has brought you out with a mighty hand, and redeemed you from the house of bondage, from the hand of Pharaoh king of Egypt.

"Therefore know that the Lord your God, He is God, the faithful God who keeps covenant and mercy for a thousand generations with those who love Him and keep His commandments." DEUTERONOMY 7:8–9

"The rainbow shall be in the cloud, and I will look on it to remember the everlasting covenant between God and every living creature of all flesh that is on the earth."

GENESIS 9:16

"Behold, this day I am going the way of all the earth. And you know in all your hearts and in all your souls that not one thing has failed of all the good things which the Lord your God spoke concerning you. All have come to pass for you, and not one word of them has failed."

JOSHUA 23:14

I will sing of the mercies of the Lord forever; with my mouth will I make known Your faithfulness to all generations.

For I have said, "Mercy shall be built up forever; Your faithfulness You shall establish in the very heavens." PSALM 89:1–2

No temptation has overtaken you except such as is common to man; but God is faithful, who will not allow you to be tempted beyond what you are able, but with the temptation will also make the way of escape, that you may be able to bear it. 1 CORINTHIANS 10:13

He will not allow your foot to be moved; He who keeps you will not slumber.

Behold, He who keeps Israel shall neither slumber nor sleep. PSALM 121:3–4

The Lord is not slack concerning His promise, as some count slackness, but is longsuffering toward us, not willing that any should perish but that all should come to repentance. 2 PETER 3:9

Victory of the Church

He has delivered us from the power of darkness and translated us into the kingdom of the Son of His love,

And He is the head of the body, the church, who is the beginning, the firstborn from the dead, that in all things He may have the preeminence. COLOSSIANS 1:13,18

He said to them, "But who do you say that I am?"

And Simon Peter answered and said, "You are the Christ, the Son of the living God."

Jesus answered and said to him, "Blessed are you, Simon Bar-Jonah, for flesh and blood has not revealed this to you, but My Father who is in heaven.

"And I also say to you that you are Peter, and on this rock I will build My church, and the gates of Hades shall not prevail against it."

MATTHEW 16:15–18

The Gentiles shall see your righteousness, and all kings your glory. You shall be called by a new name, which the mouth of the Lord will name.

You shall also be a crown of glory in the hand of the Lord, and a royal diadem in the hand of your God. ISAIAH 62:2–3

The voice of one crying in the wilderness: "Prepare the way of the Lord; make straight in the desert a highway for our God.

"Every valley shall be exalted, and every mountain and hill shall be made low; the crooked places shall be made straight, and the rough places smooth;

"The glory of the Lord shall be revealed, and all flesh shall see it together; for the mouth of the Lord has spoken." ISAIAH 40:3–5

"Behold! My Servant whom I uphold, My Elect One in whom My soul delights! I have put My Spirit upon Him; He will bring forth justice to the Gentiles.

"He will not fail nor be discouraged, till He has established justice in the earth; and the coastlands shall wait for His law." ISAIAH 42:1,4

That in the dispensation of the fullness of the times He might gather together in one all things in Christ, both which are in heaven and which are on earth—in Him.

And He put all things under His feet, and gave Him to be head over all things to the church,

which is His body, the fullness of Him who fills all in all. EPHESIANS 1:10,22–23

From whom the whole family in heaven and earth is named,

to Him be glory in the church by Christ Jesus throughout all ages, world without end. Amen. EPHESIANS 3:15,21

But I saw no temple in it, for the Lord God Almighty and the Lamb are its temple.

And the city had no need of the sun or of

the moon to shine in it, for the glory of God illuminated it, and the Lamb is its light.

And the nations of those who are saved shall walk in its light, and the kings of the earth bring their glory and honor into it.

Its gates shall not be shut at all by day (there shall be no night there).

And they shall bring the glory and the honor of the nations into it. REVELATION 21:22–26

"I, the Lord, have called You in righteousness, and will hold Your hand; I will keep You and give You as a covenant to the people, as a light to the Gentiles,

"To open blind eyes, to bring out prisoners from the prison, those who sit in darkness from the prison house." ISAIAH 42:6–7

For the husband is head of the wife, as also Christ is head of the church; and He is the Savior of the body.

Therefore, just as the church is subject to Christ, so let the wives be to their own husbands in everything.

Husbands, love your wives, just as Christ also loved the church and gave Himself for it,

that He might sanctify and cleanse it with the washing of water by the word, that He might present it to Himself a glorious church, not having spot or wrinkle or any such thing, but that it should be holy and without blemish. EPHESIANS 5:23–27

For in Him dwells all the fullness of the Godhead bodily;

And you are complete in Him, who is the head of all principality and power.

And not holding fast to the Head, from whom all the body, nourished and knit together by joints and ligaments, grows with the increase which is from God. COLOSSIANS 2:9–10,19

Having been built on the foundation of the apostles and prophets, Jesus Christ Himself being the chief cornerstone,

in whom the whole building, being joined together, grows into a holy temple in the Lord,

in whom you also are being built together for a habitation of God in the Spirit.

EPHESIANS 2:20–22

"Ask of Me, and I will give You the nations for Your inheritance, and the ends of the earth for Your possession.

"You shall break them with a rod of iron;

You shall dash them in pieces like a potter's vessel." PSALM 2:8–9

Then the Lord will be known to Egypt, and the Egyptians will know the Lord in that day, and will make sacrifice and offering; yes, they will make a vow to the Lord and perform it.

In that day Israel will be one of three with Egypt and Assyria, even a blessing in the midst of the land,

whom the Lord of hosts shall bless, saying, "Blessed is Egypt My people, and Assyria the work of My hands, and Israel My inheritance."

ISAIAH 19:19,24–25

His name shall endure forever; His name shall continue as long as the sun. And men shall be blessed in Him; all nations shall call Him blessed. PSALM 72:17

Now it shall come to pass in the latter days that the mountain of the Lord's house shall be established on the top of the mountains, and shall be exalted above the hills; and all nations shall flow to it.

Many people shall come and say, "Come, and let us go up to the mountain of the Lord, to the house of the God of Jacob; He will teach us

His ways, and we shall walk in His paths." For out of Zion shall go forth the law, and the word of the Lord from Jerusalem. ISAIAH 2:2–3

All nations whom You have made shall come and worship before You, O Lord, and shall glorify Your name. PSALM 86:9

"And in that day there shall be a Root of Jesse, who shall stand as a banner to the people; for the Gentiles shall seek Him, and His resting place shall be glorious." ISAIAH 11:10

So the nations shall fear the name of the Lord, and all the kings of the earth Your glory.
For the Lord shall build up Zion; He shall appear in His glory. PSALM 102:15–16

God's Mercy in Judgment

"Yet the number of the children of Israel shall be as the sand of the sea, which cannot be measured or numbered. And it shall come to pass in the place where it was said to them, 'You are not *My* people,' there it shall be said to them, 'You are the sons of the living God.'

"Then the children of Judah and the children

of Israel shall be gathered together, and appoint for themselves one head; and they shall come up out of the land, for great will be the day of Jezreel!" HOSEA 1:10–11

"Behold, I will bring it health and healing; I will heal them and reveal to them the abundance of peace and truth.

"And I will cause the captives of Judah and the captives of Israel to return, and will rebuild those places as at the first.

"I will cleanse them from all their iniquity by which they have sinned against Me, and I will pardon all their iniquities by which they have sinned and by which they have transgressed against Me.

"Then it shall be to Me a name of joy, a praise, and an honor before all nations of the earth, who shall hear all the good that I do to them; they shall fear and tremble for all the goodness and all the prosperity that I provide for it." JEREMIAH 33:6–9

"I will surely assemble all of you, O Jacob, I will surely gather the remnant of Israel; I will put them together like sheep of the fold, like a flock in the midst of their pasture; they shall make a loud noise because of so many men.

"The one who breaks open will come up before them; they will break out, pass through the gate, and go out by it; their king will pass before them, with the Lord at their head."

MICAH 2:12–13

Thus says the Lord: "Again there shall be heard in this place—of which you say, 'It is desolate, without man and without beast'—in the cities of Judah, in the streets of Jerusalem that are desolate, without man and without inhabitant and without beast,

"the voice of joy and the voice of gladness, the voice of the bridegroom and the voice of the bride, the voice of those who will say: 'Praise the Lord of hosts, for the Lord is good, for His mercy endures forever'—and of those who will bring the sacrifice of praise into the house of the Lord. For I will cause the captives of the land to return as at the first," says the Lord.

JEREMIAH 33:10–11

"For I will take you from among the nations, gather you out of all countries, and bring you into your own land.

"Then I will sprinkle clean water on you, and you shall be clean; I will cleanse you from all your filthiness and from all your idols.

"I will give you a new heart and put a new spirit within you; I will take the heart of stone out of your flesh and give you a heart of flesh."

EZEKIEL 36:24–26

"But on Mount Zion there shall be deliverance, and there shall be holiness; the house of Jacob shall possess their possessions.

"Then saviors shall come to Mount Zion to judge the mountains of Esau, and the kingdom shall be the Lord's." OBADIAH 17,21

For the children of Israel shall abide many days without king or prince, without sacrifice or sacred pillar, without ephod or teraphim.

Afterward the children of Israel shall return, seek the Lord their God and David their king, and fear the Lord and His goodness in the latter days. HOSEA 3:4–5

In those days Judah will be saved, and Jerusalem will dwell safely. And this is the name by which she will be called: THE LORD OUR RIGHTEOUSNESS.

For thus says the Lord: "David shall never lack a man to sit on the throne of the house of Israel." JEREMIAH 33:16–17

"For behold, in those days and at that time, when I bring back the captives of Judah and Jerusalem,

"I will also gather all nations, and bring them down to the Valley of Jehoshaphat; and I will enter into judgment with them there on account of My people, My heritage Israel, whom they have scattered among the nations; they have also divided up My land." JOEL 3:1–2

But they shall serve the Lord their God, and David their king, whom I will raise up for them.

"Therefore do not fear, O My servant Jacob," says the Lord, "nor be dismayed, O Israel; for behold, I will save you from afar, and your seed from the land of their captivity. Jacob shall return, have rest and be quiet, and no one shall make him afraid." JEREMIAH 30:9–10

For I do not desire, brethren, that you should be ignorant of this mystery, lest you should be wise in your own opinion, that hardening in part has happened to Israel until the fullness of the Gentiles has come in.

And so all Israel will be saved, as it is written: "The Deliverer will come out of Zion, and He will turn away ungodliness from Jacob;

"For this is My covenant with them, when I take away their sins." ROMANS 11:25–27

Concerning the gospel they are enemies for your sake, but concerning the election they are beloved for the sake of the fathers.

For the gifts and the calling of God are irrevocable.

For as you were once disobedient to God, yet have now obtained mercy through their disobedience,

even so these also have now been disobedient, that through the mercy shown you they also may obtain mercy.

For God has committed them all to disobedience, that He might have mercy on all.

ROMANS 11:28–32

"I will bring back the captives of My people Israel; they shall build the waste cities and inhabit them; they shall plant vineyards and drink wine from them; they shall also make gardens and eat fruit from them.

"I will plant them in their land, and no longer shall they be pulled up from the land I have given them," says the Lord your God.

AMOS 9:14–15

"So you shall know that I am the Lord your God, dwelling in Zion My holy mountain. Then Jerusalem shall be holy, and no aliens shall ever pass through her again.

"But Judah shall abide forever, and Jerusalem from generation to generation."

JOEL 3:17,20

"I will strengthen the house of Judah, and I will save the house of Joseph. I will bring them back, because I have mercy on them. They shall be as though I had not cast them aside; for I am the Lord their God, and I will hear them.

"I will whistle for them and gather them, for I will redeem them; and they shall increase as they once increased.

"I will sow them among the peoples, and they shall remember Me in far countries; they shall live, together with their children, and they shall return." ZECHARIAH 10:6,8–9

Return of Christ

For the Lord Himself will descend from heaven with a shout, with the voice of an archangel, and with the trumpet of God. And the dead in Christ will rise first.

Then we who are alive and remain shall be caught up together with them in the clouds to meet the Lord in the air. And thus we shall always be with the Lord. 1 THESSALONIANS 4:16–17

Behold, He is coming with clouds, and every eye will see Him, and they also who pierced Him. And all the tribes of the earth will mourn because of Him. Even so, Amen.

REVELATION 1:7

"And if I go and prepare a place for you, I will come again and receive you to Myself; that where I am, there you may be also." JOHN 14:3

Looking for the blessed hope and glorious appearing of our great God and Savior Jesus Christ. TITUS 2:13

So Christ was offered once to bear the sins of many. To those who eagerly wait for Him He will appear a second time, apart from sin, for salvation. HEBREWS 9:28

Therefore judge nothing before the time, until the Lord comes, who will both bring to light the hidden things of darkness and reveal the counsels of the hearts; and then each one's praise will come from God. 1 CORINTHIANS 4:5

Finally, there is laid up for me the crown of righteousness, which the Lord, the righteous Judge, will give to me on that Day, and not to me only but also to all who have loved His appearing. 2 TIMOTHY 4:8

"Then the sign of the Son of Man will appear in heaven, and then all the tribes of the earth will mourn, and they will see the Son of Man coming on the clouds of heaven with power and great glory.

"Watch therefore, for you do not know what hour your Lord is coming." MATTHEW 24:30,42

Beloved, now we are children of God; and it has not yet been revealed what we shall be, but we know that when He is revealed, we shall be like Him, for we shall see Him as He is.

1 JOHN 3:2

"You have heard Me say to you, 'I am going away and coming back to you.' If you loved Me, you would rejoice because I said, 'I am going to the Father,' for My Father is greater than I."

JOHN 14:28

And when the Chief Shepherd appears, you will receive the crown of glory that does not fade away. 1 PETER 5:4

And to wait for His Son from heaven, whom He raised from the dead, even Jesus who delivers us from the wrath to come.

1 THESSALONIANS 1:10

And Jesus said, "I am. And you will see the Son of Man sitting at the right hand of the Power, and coming with the clouds of heaven."

MARK 14:62

When Christ who is our life appears, then you also will appear with Him in glory.

COLOSSIANS 3:4

And to give you who are troubled rest with us when the Lord Jesus is revealed from heaven with His mighty angels.

2 THESSALONIANS 1:7

"For as the lightning comes from the east and flashes to the west, so also will the coming of the Son of Man be." MATTHEW 24:27

"And I will pour on the house of David and on the inhabitants of Jerusalem the Spirit of grace and supplication; then they will look on Me whom they have pierced; they will mourn for Him as one mourns for his only son, and grieve for Him as one grieves for a firstborn."

ZECHARIAH 12:10

For I know that my Redeemer lives, and He shall stand at last on the earth. JOB 19:25

And in that day His feet will stand on the Mount of Olives, which faces Jerusalem on the east. And the Mount of Olives shall be split in two, from east to west, making a very large valley; half of the mountain shall move toward the north and half of it toward the south.

ZECHARIAH 14:4

For as often as you eat this bread and drink this cup, you proclaim the Lord's death till He comes. 1 CORINTHIANS 11:26

So Christ was offered once to bear the sins of many. To those who eagerly wait for Him He will appear a second time, apart from sin, for salvation. HEBREWS 9:28

"And behold, I am coming quickly, and My reward is with Me, to give to every one according to his work."

He who testifies to these things says, "Surely I am coming quickly." Amen. Even so, come, Lord Jesus! REVELATION 22:12,20

Who also said, "Men of Galilee, why do you stand gazing up into heaven? This same Jesus, who was taken up from you into heaven, will so come in like manner as you saw Him go into heaven." ACTS 1:11

"For the Son of Man will come in the glory of His Father with His angels, and then He will reward each according to his works."

MATTHEW 16:27

"And that He may send Jesus Christ, who was preached to you before,

"whom heaven must receive until the times

of restoration of all things, which God has spoken by the mouth of all His holy prophets since the world began." ACTS 3:20–21

Increase of Knowledge and Light

❧ They shall not hurt nor destroy in all My holy mountain, for the earth shall be full of the knowledge of the Lord as the waters cover the sea. ISAIAH 11:9

"But you, Daniel, shut up the words, and seal the book until the time of the end; many shall run to and fro, and knowledge shall increase." DANIEL 12:4

How beautiful upon the mountains are the feet of him who brings good news, who proclaims peace, who brings glad tidings of good things, who proclaims salvation, who says to Zion, "Your God reigns!"

Your watchmen shall lift up their voices, with their voices they shall sing together; for they shall see eye to eye when the Lord brings back Zion.

The Lord has made bare His holy arm in the eyes of all the nations; and all the ends of the earth shall see the salvation of our God.

ISAIAH 52:7–8,10

All your children shall be taught by the Lord, and great shall be the peace of your children. ISAIAH 54:13

Oh, sing to the Lord a new song! For He has done marvelous things; His right hand and His holy arm have gained Him the victory.

The Lord has made known His salvation; His righteousness He has openly shown in the sight of the nations.

He has remembered His mercy and His faithfulness to the house of Israel; all the ends of the earth have seen the salvation of our God.

PSALM 98:1–3

In that day the deaf shall hear the words of the book, and the eyes of the blind shall see out of obscurity and out of darkness. ISAIAH 29:18

And in this mountain the Lord of hosts will make for all people a feast of choice pieces, a feast of wines on the lees, of fat things full of marrow, of well-refined wines on the lees.

And He will destroy on this mountain the surface of the covering cast over all people, and the veil that is spread over all nations.

ISAIAH 25:6–7

Behold, is it not of the Lord of hosts that the peoples labor to feed the fire, and nations weary themselves in vain?

For the earth will be filled with the knowledge of the glory of the Lord, as the waters cover the sea. HABAKKUK 2:13–14

"These also who erred in spirit will come to understanding, and those who murmured will learn doctrine." ISAIAH 29:24

Then the lame shall leap like a deer, and the tongue of the dumb sing. For waters shall burst forth in the wilderness, and streams in the desert.

The parched ground shall become a pool, and the thirsty land springs of water; in the habitation of jackals, where each lay, there shall be grass with reeds and rushes.

A highway shall be there, and a road, and it shall be called the Highway of Holiness. The unclean shall not pass over it, but it shall be for others. Whoever walks the road, although a fool, shall not go astray.

No lion shall be there, nor shall any ravenous beast go up on it; it shall not be found there. But the redeemed shall walk there,

And the ransomed of the Lord shall return, and come to Zion with singing, with everlasting joy on their heads. They shall obtain joy and gladness, and sorrow and sighing shall flee away. ISAIAH 35:6–10

How beautiful upon the mountains are the feet of him who brings good news, who proclaims peace, who brings glad tidings of good things, who proclaims salvation, who says to Zion, "Your God reigns!"

Your watchmen shall lift up their voices, with their voices they shall sing together; for they shall see eye to eye when the Lord brings back Zion. ISAIAH 52:7–8

"For I know their works and their thoughts. It shall be that I will gather all nations and tongues; and they shall come and see My glory.

"I will set a sign among them; and those among them who escape I will send to the nations: to Tarshish and Pul and Lud, who draw the bow, and Tubal and Javan, to the coastlands afar off who have not heard My fame nor seen My glory. And they shall declare My glory among the Gentiles." ISAIAH 66:18–19

"The sun shall no longer be your light by day, nor for brightness shall the moon give light to you; but the Lord will be to you an everlasting light, and your God your glory.

"Your sun shall no longer go down, nor shall your moon withdraw itself; for the Lord will be your everlasting light, and the days of your mourning shall be ended.

"Also your people shall all be righteous; they shall inherit the land forever, the branch of My planting, the work of My hands, that I may be glorified." ISAIAH 60:19–21

Ultimate Peace

"The wolf also shall dwell with the lamb, the leopard shall lie down with the young goat, the calf and the young lion and the fatling together; and a little child shall lead them.

"The cow and the bear shall graze; their young ones shall lie down together; and the lion shall eat straw like the ox.

"The nursing child shall play by the cobra's hole, and the weaned child shall put his hand in the viper's den.

"They shall not hurt nor destroy in all My holy mountain, for the earth shall be full of the knowledge of the Lord as the waters cover the sea." ISAIAH 11:6–9

Give the king Your judgments, O God, and Your righteousness to the king's Son.

He will judge Your people with righteousness, and Your poor with justice.

The mountains will bring peace to the people, and the little hills, by righteousness.

PSALM 72:1–3

He shall judge between the nations, and shall rebuke many people; they shall beat their swords into plowshares, and their spears into pruning hooks; nation shall not lift up sword against nation, neither shall they learn war anymore. ISAIAH 2:4

Thus says the Lord, the Redeemer of Israel, their Holy One, to Him whom man despises, to Him whom the nation abhors, to the Servant of rulers: "Kings shall see and arise, princes also shall worship, because of the Lord who is faithful, the Holy One of Israel; and He has chosen You.

"Kings shall be your foster fathers, and their queens your nursing mothers; they shall bow down to you with their faces to the earth, and lick up the dust of your feet. Then you will know that I am the Lord, for they shall not be ashamed who wait for Me." ISAIAH 49:7,23

He will bring justice to the poor of the people; He will save the children of the needy, and will break in pieces the oppressor.

They shall fear You as long as the sun and moon endure, throughout all generations.

He shall come down like rain upon the mown grass, like showers that water the earth.

PSALM 72:4–6

In those days Judah will be saved, and Jerusalem will dwell safely. And this is the name by which she will be called: THE LORD OUR RIGHTEOUSNESS. JEREMIAH 33:16

He shall have dominion also from sea to sea, and from the River to the ends of the earth.

Yes, all kings shall fall down before Him; all nations shall serve Him.

He will spare the poor and needy, and will save the souls of the needy.

He will redeem their life from oppression and violence; and precious shall be their blood in His sight. PSALM 72:8,11,13–14

Then the Lord will create above every dwelling place of Mount Zion, and above her assemblies, a cloud and smoke by day and the shining of a flaming fire by night. For over all the glory there will be a covering.

And there will be a tabernacle for shade in the daytime from the heat, for a place of refuge, and for a shelter from storm and rain.

ISAIAH 4:5–6

But be glad and rejoice forever in what I create; for behold, I create Jerusalem as a rejoicing, and her people a joy.

I will rejoice in Jerusalem, and joy in My people; the voice of weeping shall no longer be heard in her, nor the voice of crying.

ISAIAH 65:18–19

"Whereas you have been forsaken and hated, so that no one went through you, I will make you an eternal excellence, a joy of many generations.

"You shall drink dry the milk of the Gentiles, and shall milk the breast of kings; you shall know that I, the Lord, am your Savior and your Redeemer, the Mighty One of Jacob.

"Instead of bronze I will bring gold, instead of iron I will bring silver, instead of wood, bronze, and instead of stones, iron. I will also make your officers peace, and your magistrates righteousness.

"Violence shall no longer be heard in your land, neither wasting nor destruction within your borders; but you shall call your walls Salvation, and your gates Praise." ISAIAH 60:15–18

Destruction of Evil

The Lord shall send the rod of Your strength out of Zion. Rule in the midst of Your enemies!

The Lord is at Your right hand; He shall execute kings in the day of His wrath.

He shall judge among the nations, He shall fill the places with dead bodies, He shall execute the heads of many countries.

PSALM 110:2,5–6

But with righteousness He shall judge the poor, and decide with equity for the meek of the earth; He shall strike the earth with the rod of His mouth, and with the breath of His lips He shall slay the wicked. ISAIAH 11:4

"Behold, all those who were incensed against you shall be ashamed and disgraced; they shall be as nothing, and those who strive with you shall perish.

"You shall seek them and not find them—those who contended with you. Those who war against you shall be as nothing, as a nonexistent thing." ISAIAH 41:11–12

So shall they fear the name of the Lord from the west, and His glory from the rising of the sun; when the enemy comes in like a flood, the Spirit of the Lord will lift up a standard against him. ISAIAH 59:19

Shall the prey be taken from the mighty, or the captives of the righteous be delivered?

But thus says the Lord: "Even the captives of the mighty shall be taken away, and the prey of the terrible be delivered; for I will contend with him who contends with you, and I will save your children.

"I will feed those who oppress you with their own flesh, and they shall be drunk with their own blood as with sweet wine. All flesh shall know that I, the Lord, am your Savior, and your Redeemer, the Mighty One of Jacob."

ISAIAH 49:24–26

Also the sons of those who afflicted you shall come bowing to you, and all those who despised you shall fall prostrate at the soles of your feet; and they shall call you The City of the Lord, Zion of the Holy One of Israel. ISAIAH 60:14

And then the lawless one will be revealed, whom the Lord will consume with the breath of His mouth and destroy with the brightness of His coming. 2 THESSALONIANS 2:8

"The ten horns are ten kings who shall arise from this kingdom. And another shall rise after them; he shall be different from the first ones, and shall subdue three kings.

"He shall speak pompous words against the Most High, shall persecute the saints of the Most High, and shall intend to change times and law. Then the saints shall be given into his hand for a time and times and half a time.

"But the court shall be seated, and they shall take away his dominion, to consume and destroy it forever." DANIEL 7:24–26

Then a third angel followed them, saying with a loud voice, "If anyone worships the beast and his image, and receives his mark on his forehead or on his hand,

"he himself shall also drink of the wine of the wrath of God, which is poured out full strength into the cup of His indignation. And he shall be tormented with fire and brimstone in the presence of the holy angels and in the presence of the Lamb." REVELATION 14:9–10

For thus says the Lord God: "When I make you a desolate city, like cities that are not inhabited, when I bring the deep upon you, and great waters cover you.

"I will make you a terror, and you shall be no more; though you are sought for, you will never be found again," says the Lord God.

EZEKIEL 26:19,21

And he cried mightily with a loud voice, saying, "Babylon the great is fallen, is fallen, and has become a habitation of demons, a prison for every foul spirit, and a cage for every unclean and hated bird!"

"Therefore her plagues will come in one day—death and mourning and famine. And she will be utterly burned with fire, for strong is the Lord God who judges her.

"Rejoice over her, O heaven, and you holy apostles and prophets, for God has avenged you on her!" REVELATION 18:2,8,20

And I saw the beast, the kings of the earth, and their armies, gathered together to make war against Him who sat on the horse and against His army.

Then the beast was captured, and with him

the false prophet who worked signs in his presence, by which he deceived those who received the mark of the beast and those who worshiped his image. These two were cast alive into the lake of fire burning with brimstone.

REVELATION 19:19–20

Now when the thousand years have expired, Satan will be released from his prison

and will go out to deceive the nations which are in the four corners of the earth, Gog and Magog, to gather them together to battle, whose number is as the sand of the sea.

They went up on the breadth of the earth and surrounded the camp of the saints and the beloved city. And fire came down from God out of heaven and devoured them. REVELATION 20:7–9

In that day the Lord with His severe sword, great and strong, will punish Leviathan the fleeing serpent, Leviathan that twisted serpent; and He will slay the reptile that is in the sea.

ISAIAH 27:1

"And I will bring him to judgment with pestilence and bloodshed; I will rain down on him, on his troops, and on the many peoples who are with him, flooding rain, great hailstones, fire, and brimstone.

"Thus I will magnify Myself and sanctify Myself, and I will be known in the eyes of many nations. Then they shall know that I am the Lord." EZEKIEL 38:22–23

PROMISES OF AN ETERNAL FUTURE

A Glorious Resurrection

❧ Jesus said to her, "I am the resurrection and the life. He who believes in Me, though he may die, he shall live." JOHN 11:25

And many of those who sleep in the dust of the earth shall awake, some to everlasting life, some to shame and everlasting contempt.

DANIEL 12:2

For we know that if our earthly house, this tent, is destroyed, we have a building from God, a house not made with hands, eternal in the heavens.

For in this we groan, earnestly desiring to be clothed with our habitation which is from heaven,

if indeed, having been clothed, we shall not be found naked.

For we who are in this tent groan, being burdened, not because we want to be unclothed, but further clothed, that mortality may be swallowed up by life. 2 CORINTHIANS 5:1–4

"Do not marvel at this; for the hour is coming in which all who are in the graves will hear His voice

"and come forth—those who have done good, to the resurrection of life, and those who have done evil, to the resurrection of condemnation." JOHN 5:28–29

Your dead shall live; together with my dead body they shall arise. Awake and sing, you who dwell in dust; for your dew is like the dew of herbs, and the earth shall cast out the dead.

ISAIAH 26:19

Therefore my heart is glad, and my glory rejoices; My flesh also will rest in hope.

For You will not leave my soul in Sheol, nor will You allow Your Holy One to see corruption. PSALM 16:9–10

And after my skin is destroyed, this I know, that in my flesh I shall see God,

Whom I shall see for myself, and my eyes shall behold, and not another. How my heart yearns within me! JOB 19:26–27

For since by man came death, by Man also came the resurrection of the dead.

1 CORINTHIANS 15:21

"But those who are counted worthy to attain that age, and the resurrection from the dead, neither marry nor are given in marriage;

"nor can they die anymore, for they are equal to the angels and are sons of God, being sons of the resurrection." LUKE 20:35–36

But if the Spirit of Him who raised Jesus from the dead dwells in you, He who raised Christ from the dead will also give life to your mortal bodies through His Spirit who dwells in you. ROMANS 8:11

So also is the resurrection of the dead. The body is sown in corruption, it is raised in incorruption.

It is sown in dishonor, it is raised in glory. It is sown in weakness, it is raised in power.

It is sown a natural body, it is raised a spiritual body. There is a natural body, and there is a spiritual body. 1 CORINTHIANS 15:42–44

Knowing that He who raised up the Lord Jesus will also raise us up with Jesus, and will present us with you. 2 CORINTHIANS 4:14

Who will transform our lowly body that it may be conformed to His glorious body, according to the working by which He is able even to subdue all things to Himself.

PHILIPPIANS 3:21

And as we have borne the image of the man of dust, we shall also bear the image of the heavenly Man.

Now this I say, brethren, that flesh and blood cannot inherit the kingdom of God; nor does corruption inherit incorruption.

Behold, I tell you a mystery: We shall not all sleep, but we shall all be changed—

in a moment, in the twinkling of an eye, at the last trumpet. For the trumpet will sound, and the dead will be raised incorruptible, and we shall be changed.

For this corruptible must put on incorruption, and this mortal must put on immortality.

So when this corruptible has put on incorruption, and this mortal has put on immortality, then shall be brought to pass the saying that is written: "Death is swallowed up in victory." 1 CORINTHIANS 15:49–54

For if we believe that Jesus died and rose again, even so God will bring with Him those who sleep in Jesus.

For this we say to you by the word of the Lord, that we who are alive and remain until the coming of the Lord will by no means precede those who are asleep.

For the Lord Himself will descend from heaven with a shout, with the voice of an archangel, and with the trumpet of God. And the dead in Christ will rise first.

Then we who are alive and remain shall be caught up together with them in the clouds to meet the Lord in the air. And thus we shall always be with the Lord. 1 THESSALONIANS 4:14–17

Eternal Life

And this is the promise that He has promised us—eternal life. 1 JOHN 2:25

"Most assuredly, I say to you, he who believes in Me has everlasting life." JOHN 6:47

Jesus said to her, "I am the resurrection and the life. He who believes in Me, though he may die, he shall live.

"And whoever lives and believes in Me shall never die. Do you believe this?" JOHN 11:25–26

But now having been set free from sin, and having become slaves of God, you have your fruit to holiness, and the end, everlasting life.

For the wages of sin is death, but the gift of God is eternal life in Christ Jesus our Lord.

ROMANS 6:22–23

For he who sows to his flesh will of the flesh reap corruption, but he who sows to the Spirit will of the Spirit reap everlasting life.

GALATIANS 6:8

"My sheep hear My voice, and I know them, and they follow Me.

"And I give them eternal life, and they shall never perish; neither shall anyone snatch them out of My hand." JOHN 10:27–28

"I am the living bread which came down from heaven. If anyone eats of this bread, he will live forever; and the bread that I shall give is My flesh, which I shall give for the life of the world."

"Whoever eats My flesh and drinks My blood has eternal life, and I will raise him up at the last day." JOHN 6:51,54

"And these will go away into everlasting punishment, but the righteous into eternal life."

MATTHEW 25:46

"Nor can they die anymore, for they are equal to the angels and are sons of God, being sons of the resurrection." LUKE 20:36

In hope of eternal life which God, who cannot lie, promised before time began.

TITUS 1:2

And this is the testimony: that God has given us eternal life, and this life is in His Son.

These things I have written to you who believe in the name of the Son of God, that you may know that you have eternal life, and that you may continue to believe in the name of the Son of God. 1 JOHN 5:11,13

"For God so loved the world that He gave His only begotten Son, that whoever believes in Him should not perish but have everlasting life."

JOHN 3:16

"But whoever drinks of the water that I shall give him will never thirst. But the water that I shall give him will become in him a fountain of water springing up into everlasting life." JOHN 4:14

"Most assuredly, I say to you, he who hears My word and believes in Him who sent Me has everlasting life, and shall not come into judgment, but has passed from death into life."

JOHN 5:24

"Do not labor for the food which perishes, but for the food which endures to everlasting life, which the Son of Man will give you, because God the Father has set His seal on Him."

JOHN 6:27

"As you have given Him authority over all flesh, that He should give eternal life to as many as You have given Him." JOHN 17:2

"That having been justified by His grace we should become heirs according to the hope of eternal life." TITUS 3:7

And we know that the Son of God has come and has given us an understanding, that we may know Him who is true; and we are in Him who is true, in His Son Jesus Christ. This is the true God and eternal life. 1 JOHN 5:20

An Everlasting Inheritance

And for this reason He is the Mediator of the new covenant, by means of death, for the redemption of the transgressions under the first covenant, that those who are called may receive the promise of the eternal inheritance.

HEBREWS 9:15

Blessed be the God and Father of our Lord Jesus Christ, who according to His abundant mercy has begotten us again to a living hope through the resurrection of Jesus Christ from the dead,

to an inheritance incorruptible and undefiled and that does not fade away, reserved in heaven for you. 1 PETER 1:3–4

The eyes of your understanding being enlightened; that you may know what is the hope of His calling, what are the riches of the glory of His inheritance in the saints.

EPHESIANS 1:18

"He who overcomes shall inherit all things, and I will be his God and he shall be My son."

REVELATION 21:7

"And I bestow upon you a kingdom, just as My Father bestowed one upon Me,

"that you may eat and drink at My table in My kingdom, and sit on thrones judging the twelve tribes of Israel." LUKE 22:29–30

And the Lord will deliver me from every evil work and preserve me for His heavenly kingdom. To Him be glory forever and ever. Amen! 2 TIMOTHY 4:18

"Then the King will say to those on His right hand, 'Come, you blessed of My Father, inherit the kingdom prepared for you from the foundation of the world.'" MATTHEW 25:34

But as it is written: "Eye has not seen, nor ear heard, nor have entered into the heart of man the things which God has prepared for those who love Him." 1 CORINTHIANS 2:9

For so an entrance will be supplied to you abundantly into the everlasting kingdom of our Lord and Savior Jesus Christ. 2 PETER 1:11

"Do not fear, little flock, for it is your Father's good pleasure to give you the kingdom." LUKE 12:32

And if children, then heirs—heirs of God and joint heirs with Christ, if indeed we suffer with Him, that we may also be glorified together.

For I consider that the sufferings of this present time are not worthy to be compared with the glory which shall be revealed in us.

ROMANS 8:17–18

"But lay up for yourselves treasures in heaven, where neither moth nor rust destroys and where thieves do not break in and steal."

MATTHEW 6:20

"His lord said to him, 'Well done, good and faithful servant; you were faithful over a few things, I will make you ruler over many things. Enter into the joy of your lord.'" MATTHEW 25:21

Beloved, now we are children of God; and it has not yet been revealed what we shall be, but we know that when He is revealed, we shall be like Him, for we shall see Him as He is.

1 JOHN 3:2

Receiving the end of your faith—the salvation of your souls.

Therefore gird up the loins of your mind, be sober, and rest your hope fully upon the grace that is to be brought to you at the revelation of Jesus Christ. 1 PETER 1:9,13

"In My Father's house are many mansions; if it were not so, I would have told you. I go to prepare a place for you.

"And if I go and prepare a place for you, I

will come again and receive you to Myself; that where I am, there you may be also." JOHN 14:2–3

Your sun shall no longer go down, nor shall your moon withdraw itself; for the Lord will be your everlasting light, and the days of your mourning shall be ended.

Also your people shall all be righteous; they shall inherit the land forever, the branch of My planting, the work of My hands, that I may be glorified. ISAIAH 60:20–21

A Home With God

"In My Father's house are many mansions; if it were not so, I would have told you. I go to prepare a place for you.

"And if I go and prepare a place for you, I will come again and receive you to Myself; that where I am, there you may be also.

"And where I go you know, and the way you know." JOHN 14:2–4

Surely goodness and mercy shall follow me all the days of my life; and I will dwell in the house of the Lord forever. PSALM 23:6

By faith he sojourned in the land of promise as in a foreign country, dwelling in tents with Isaac and Jacob, the heirs with him of the same promise;

for he waited for the city which has foundations, whose builder and maker is God.

But now they desire a better, that is, a heavenly country. Therefore God is not ashamed to be called their God, for He has prepared a city for them. HEBREWS 11:9–10,16

And I saw a new heaven and a new earth, for the first heaven and the first earth had passed away. Also there was no more sea.

Then I, John, saw the holy city, New Jerusalem, coming down out of heaven from God, prepared as a bride adorned for her husband. REVELATION 21:1–2

But I saw no temple in it, for the Lord God Almighty and the Lamb are its temple.

REVELATION 21:22

Nevertheless we, according to His promise, look for new heavens and a new earth in which righteousness dwells. 2 PETER 3:13

And Jesus said to him, "Assuredly, I say to you, today you will be with Me in Paradise."
LUKE 23:43

For to me, to live is Christ, and to die is gain.

For I am hard pressed between the two, having a desire to depart and be with Christ, which is far better. PHILIPPIANS 1:21,23

For we know that if our earthly house, this tent, is destroyed, we have a building from God, a house not made with hands, eternal in the heavens.

For in this we groan, earnestly desiring to be clothed with our habitation which is from heaven,

if indeed, having been clothed, we shall not be found naked.

For we who are in this tent groan, being burdened, not because we want to be unclothed, but further clothed, that mortality may be swallowed up by life. 2 CORINTHIANS 5:1–4

There remains therefore a rest for the people of God. HEBREWS 4:9

Unending Happiness

But as it is written: "Eye has not seen, nor ear heard, nor have entered into the heart of man the things which God has prepared for those who love Him." 1 CORINTHIANS 2:9

For if when we were enemies we were reconciled to God through the death of His Son, much more, having been reconciled, we shall be saved by His life.

For if by the one man's offense death reigned through the one, much more those who receive abundance of grace and of the gift of righteousness will reign in life through the One, Jesus Christ. ROMANS 5:10,17

Which is manifest evidence of the righteous judgment of God, that you may be counted worthy of the kingdom of God, for which you also suffer.

And to give you who are troubled rest with us when the Lord Jesus is revealed from heaven with His mighty angels.

2 THESSALONIANS 1:5,7

There remains therefore a rest for the people of God. HEBREWS 4:9

Beloved, now we are children of God; and it has not yet been revealed what we shall be, but we know that when He is revealed, we shall be like Him, for we shall see Him as He is.

1 JOHN 3:2

Nevertheless we, according to His promise, look for new heavens and a new earth in which righteousness dwells. 2 PETER 3:13

"You have a few names even in Sardis who have not defiled their garments; and they shall walk with Me in white, for they are worthy."

REVELATION 3:4

But rejoice to the extent that you partake of Christ's sufferings, that when His glory is revealed, you may also be glad with exceeding joy. 1 PETER 4:13

Like sheep they are laid in the grave; death shall feed on them; the upright shall have dominion over them in the morning; and their beauty shall be consumed in the grave, far from their dwelling.

But God will redeem my soul from the power of the grave, for He shall receive me.

PSALM 49:14–15

And there shall be no more curse, but the throne of God and of the Lamb shall be in it, and His servants shall serve Him.

REVELATION 22:3

Your sun shall no longer go down, nor shall your moon withdraw itself; for the Lord will be your everlasting light, and the days of your mourning shall be ended. ISAIAH 60:20

"Do not fear any of those things which you are about to suffer. Indeed, the devil is about to throw some of you into prison, that you may be tested, and you will have tribulation ten days. Be faithful until death, and I will give you the crown of life." REVELATION 2:10

And God will wipe away every tear from their eyes; there shall be no more death, nor sorrow, nor crying; and there shall be no more pain, for the former things have passed away.

REVELATION 21:4

And there shall be no night there: They need no lamp nor light of the sun, for the Lord God gives them light. And they shall reign forever and ever. REVELATION 22:5

The sun shall no longer be your light by day, nor for brightness shall the moon give light to you; but the Lord will be to you an everlasting light, and your God your glory.

Your sun shall no longer go down, nor shall your moon withdraw itself; for the Lord will be your everlasting light, and the days of your mourning shall be ended. ISAIAH 60:19–20

But I saw no temple in it, for the Lord God Almighty and the Lamb are its temple.

And the city had no need of the sun or of the moon to shine in it, for the glory of God illuminated it, and the Lamb is its light.

REVELATION 21:22–23

"Therefore they are before the throne of God, and serve Him day and night in His temple. And He who sits on the throne will dwell among them.

"They shall neither hunger anymore nor

thirst anymore; the sun shall not strike them, nor any heat;

"for the Lamb who is in the midst of the throne will shepherd them and lead them to living fountains of waters. And God will wipe away every tear from their eyes."

REVELATION 7:15–17

Now to Him who is able to keep you from stumbling, and to present you faultless before the presence of His glory with exceeding joy.

JUDE 24

You will show me the path of life; in Your presence is fullness of joy; at Your right hand are pleasures forevermore. PSALM 16:11

Everlasting Glory

When Christ who is our life appears, then you also will appear with Him in glory.

COLOSSIANS 3:4

And if children, then heirs—heirs of God and joint heirs with Christ, if indeed we suffer with Him, that we may also be glorified together.

For I consider that the sufferings of this present time are not worthy to be compared with the glory which shall be revealed in us.

ROMANS 8:17–18

For our light affliction, which is but for a moment, is working for us a far more exceeding and eternal weight of glory,

while we do not look at the things which are seen, but at the things which are not seen. For the things which are seen are temporary, but the things which are not seen are eternal.

2 CORINTHIANS 4:17–18

"Then the righteous will shine forth as the sun in the kingdom of their Father. He who has ears to hear, let him hear!" MATTHEW 13:43

"And the glory which You gave Me I have given them, that they may be one just as We are one.

"Father, I desire that they also whom You gave Me may be with Me where I am, that they may behold My glory which You have given Me; for You loved Me before the foundation of the world." JOHN 17:22,24

Those who are wise shall shine like the brightness of the firmament, and those who turn many to righteousness like the stars forever and ever. DANIEL 12:3

Jesus spoke these words, lifted up His eyes to heaven, and said: "Father, the hour has come. Glorify Your Son, that Your Son also may glorify You.

"And the glory which You gave Me I have given them, that they may be one just as We are one:

"I in them, and You in Me; that they may be made perfect in one, and that the world may know that You have sent Me, and have loved them as You have loved Me." JOHN 17:1,22–23

Whose minds the god of this age has blinded, who do not believe, lest the light of the gospel of the glory of Christ, who is the image of God, should shine on them. 2 CORINTHIANS 4:4

For our citizenship is in heaven, from which we also eagerly wait for the Savior, the Lord Jesus Christ,

who will transform our lowly body that it may be conformed to His glorious body, according to the working by which He is able even to subdue all things to Himself.

PHILIPPIANS 3:20–21

Who "will render to each one according to his deeds":

eternal life to those who by patient continuance in doing good seek for glory, honor, and immortality. ROMANS 2:6–7

And one cried to another and said: "Holy, holy, holy is the Lord of hosts; the whole earth is full of His glory!" ISAIAH 6:3

The Gentiles shall see your righteousness, and all kings your glory. You shall be called by a new name, which the mouth of the Lord will name.

You shall also be a crown of glory in the hand of the Lord, and a royal diadem in the hand of your God. ISAIAH 62:2–3

Lift up your heads, O you gates! and be lifted up, you everlasting doors! And the King of glory shall come in. PSALM 24:7

"For I know their works and their thoughts. It shall be that I will gather all nations and tongues; and they shall come and see My glory.

"I will set a sign among them; and those among them who escape I will send to the nations: to Tarshish and Pul and Lud, who draw the bow, and Tubal and Javan, to the coastlands afar off who have not heard My fame nor seen My glory. And they shall declare My glory among the Gentiles." ISAIAH 66:18–19

"And now, O Father, glorify Me together with Yourself, with the glory which I had with You before the world was." JOHN 17:5

Plan of Salvation

- You Are a Sinner . . .

  As it is written: "There is none righteous, no, not one." ROMANS 3:10

- There Is a Price to be Paid for Sin . . .

  For all have sinned and fall short of the glory of God. ROMANS 3:23

- Need to Repent . . .

  "But go and learn what this means: 'I desire mercy and not sacrifice.' For I did not come to call the righteous, but sinners, to repentance."

  MATTHEW 9:13

  "I tell you, no; but unless you repent you will all likewise perish." LUKE 13:3

- God Loves You . . .

  "For God so loved the world that He gave His only begotten Son, that whoever believes in Him should not perish but have everlasting life."

  JOHN 3:16

- Christ Died for You and Wants to Save You . . .

  For the wages of sin is death, but the gift of God is eternal life in Christ Jesus our Lord.

  ROMANS 6:23

But God demonstrates His own love toward us, in that while we were still sinners, Christ died for us. ROMANS 5:8

- Christ Will Save You Now . . .

If you confess with your mouth the Lord Jesus and believe in your heart that God has raised Him from the dead, you will be saved.

For with the heart one believes to righteousness, and with the mouth confession is made to salvation. ROMANS 10:9–10

For "whoever calls upon the name of the Lord shall be saved." ROMANS 10:13

- You Can Know That You Are Saved . . .

He who believes in the Son of God has the witness in himself; he who does not believe God has made Him a liar, because he has not believed the testimony that God has given of His Son.

And this is the testimony: that God has given us eternal life, and this life is in His Son.

He who has the Son has life; he who does not have the Son of God does not have life.

These things I have written to you who believe in the name of the Son of God, that you may know that you have eternal life and that you may continue to believe in the name of the Son of God. 1 JOHN 5:10–13

Notes

Notes

Notes

Notes

Notes